After The Game

CHALLENGES FOR THE RETIRING PRO ATHLETE

Part of The Pro's Process™ Series

By Chris R. Moynes

Enjoy the Read + Dream Big!

This publication is designed to provide accurate and authoritative though general information in regard to the subject matter covered. It is not intended to provide a basis for action in particular circumstances without prior consultation with a competent professional. While every effort has been made to compile the material from reliable sources, no warranty can be made as to its completeness or accuracy.

It is distributed with the understanding that neither the author nor the publisher is engaged in offering legal, accounting, tax or other professional service. If legal, tax, accounting or other expert assistance is required, the services of a qualified and competent professional should be sought.

ISBN: 978-0-9920714-4-8

Managing Editor
Dr. Riley Moynes

Book Design
Awarewolf Creative | Jackie Duys-Kelly

Library and Archives Canada Cataloguing in Publication
Moynes, Chris, 1971-, author
          After the game : challenges for the retiring pro athlete
/ Chris R. Moynes.

(Pro's process series)
ISBN 978-0-9920714-4-8 (paperback)

1. Professional athletes--Canada--Finance, Personal.
2. Professional athletes--Retirement--Canada. I. Title.

 GV706.8.M687 2016   332.02   C2016-901286-7

Published by TMC Press

Printed and bound in Canada

Table of Contents

Dedication

This book is dedicated to the memory of my dear friend Steven R. Montador (1980-2015).

The idea was born on a grey Saturday morning in February, 2015. Monty had come to see my son Charlie play his house league hockey game, and to the excitement of all the little guys in the dressing room, he came in after the game to congratulate them and sign a bunch of autographs. He always took time for the kids.

After the game, he came back to the house to talk. He opened up to me about the many personal difficulties he was encountering, which had been brought on as a result of two main factors. First were the tangible and obvious results of the several documented concussions he'd suffered during his career. His decision-making abilities and his short-term memory had suffered noticeably in the previous year or so; he'd had several keys made for the same lock, and he had several passports because he kept losing and later re-finding them.

Second was the frustration he was feeling in attempting to find his "next life" after retirement from the game in 2013. He was depressed, he believed he'd been discarded after 12 years as a professional hockey player. He knew he needed help and guidance, but felt little had been made available from the National Hockey League Players Association (NHLPA).

He'd been exploring several work options; we discussed a number of the possibilities he was pursuing. These included hockey-related media work, coaching or scouting positions, even some connection with the NHLPA where he might help others who were facing the same struggles he was. But to date, none of these had panned out.

During our discussion, we hit on the topic of him writing a book in which he'd discuss his situation and his challenges. That was the thing about Monty; everything he did was with the thought of, "How can I give back? How can I pay it forward?" He wanted to write a book in the hope that it might be of assistance to other players who were facing the same daunting scenario in the transition from their pro careers to life after hockey.

He seemed intrigued by the idea, and said he'd like to think about it; we'd discuss it further in the coming months. One week later, on Sunday, February 15th 2015, he was gone.

After he passed, the need for such a book became even more obvious to me, so I decided to move ahead with the research project, and this publication. I'm certain that Monty would be pleased, knowing that it will be of help to others as they move close to the end of their careers and into the rest of their lives. Monty is gone but will never be forgotten; his wish to pay it forward and help others is the driving force behind this project.

DREAM BIG!

Foreword

It's 2001, Game 3 of the Stanley Cup playoff. We are up two games to nothing over the heavily favored Ottawa Senators, but they have just scored two quick goals to tie the game in its dying minutes. We sit quietly in the Toronto Maple Leaf dressing room anxiously awaiting overtime, wondering if we have wakened the sleeping giant. As we head back to the ice, the sellout Toronto crowd hollers and screams its support. A few minutes into OT, I wind up for a slap shot from the blue line; all the years of practice come together as I catch it perfectly. Like a laser, it's in the net...and the place goes wild. As I shoot, I'm hit hard... and everything goes black.

Fast forward to 2008. It's 6 am, the alarm goes off and as I wake and the fog lifts from my brain, I am reminded that I'm lying in a flea-bitten Drumheller motel with all my clothes on, and I have to get up to go to work. I'm here to try to keep a struggling trucking company in which I'm an investor afloat, a business about which I know next to nothing. But with the 2008 economic downturn and the decline in oil and gas prices, we decided we had to close this part of our business down, and concentrate all our efforts in our Lloydminster operation. (Fortunately, it survived and thrives today.) But how the hell did I end up in Drumheller? Only a few years earlier, I had been playing in the NHL, staying in five-star hotels, playing in front of thousands, signing autographs, and earning a solid NHL salary.

An aging body, a bad back, and the 2004-2005 NHL lockout all caused me to start looking at what I was going to do after hockey. Unlike a lot of guys I played with I had a university degree, and with my practical approach to life, I knew that my hockey career wouldn't last forever. So when the lockout occurred, I invested in a small oilfield service company, and qualified for my real estate license. I was determined to have options, and as I tell every kid who wants to be a pro hockey player, "Always have options. As one door closes, be prepared to step through the next one." I didn't know exactly what I'd end up doing, but I was determined to have options available. Two years later the lockout was a distant memory, and my pro hockey career was over...no one wanted me any more. But I had a new career in the oil patch, and I've never looked back.

So while I'd never discourage any aspiring player from chasing their dream, Chris' book points out the real and traumatic challenges that face every pro athlete when their career is over. I don't believe there has ever been a book written that goes into this depth, interviewing not only retired players, but also their spouses. It should be read by aspiring players, current and retiring pros, their spouses and their families. The experiences documented here are sometimes raw, but they present a very accurate picture of the opportunities and the challenges that face every retiring pro athlete.

I'm happy to know Chris as a friend and an advisor, and I'm glad he has taken on this project in an effort to help players as they transition to their lives... after the game.

Cory Cross

Cory is a 15-year veteran who played over 600 games with six NHL teams.

Introduction

"A lot of guys wish they could get back where they were, but that's the first thing that has to stop. And once you realize that all the things that allowed you to play your sport at the highest level—all the discipline and commitment and perseverance and talent will serve you well after you retire—you're ready to start training for the new season. It's the one called 'the rest of your life.'" Sean Avery, an 11-year NHL player

"Everyone says you have to get ready financially. No, no. You've got to get ready psychologically." Lee Iacocca, former Chairman of Chrysler Corporation

In my first book, entitled *The Pro's Process: An Expert's Approach to Wealth Management for Professional Athletes*, I wrote that as a professional athlete, you occupy a unique position in society. During your career, you're at the peak of the profession you've chosen, one to which you have devoted years of concentrated effort and practice. You're a role model to thousands (if not millions) of kids and adults. You command a salary that makes the average Canadian's mouth water—an average of about $2.4 million per season—and you'll earn about $13 million during your career. According to spotac.com though, 200 of the 683 players in their NHL database earn less than $1 million (US) per year, so the $13 million average income reported is heavily skewed by the top 10 salary earners in the league. It probably means you're going to have to find work after you retire, and that's the NHL. Salaries in the AHL average only about $100,000 (US) annually.

We know too that between 70% and 90% of a pro athlete's lifetime earnings will be earned before they're 35 years old.[1] So where will the money come from to support you for the remaining nearly 50 years (average Canadian life expectancy in 2015 was 82 years) of your life?

Your professional (hockey) career will average only about 5.5 years (the median is 4 years[2]), and it could end with the next play.

Most other successful professionals don't reach their highest salary-earning years until their 50s; you achieved it much earlier. You enjoy the best of everything: equipment, facilities, coaching, medical services, diet, travel. You live a lifestyle we usually associate with a rock star, or an A-list Hollywood actor. And if you play your cards right, you'll have tremendous opportunities available to you after your professional career is over.

But I noted too, that you also face some serious challenges. Your professional (hockey) career will average only about 5.5 years (the median is 4 years[2]), and it could end with the next play.

There's about a 70% chance that you will file for bankruptcy or face serious financial pressure within five years of retiring from your sport.[3]

Then, based on the staggering statistics, there's about a 70% chance that you will file for bankruptcy or face serious financial pressure within five years of retiring from your sport.[3]

1. Athlete's Financial Handbook, 2009   2. Quanthockey.com
3. How and Why Athletes Go Broke"—Sports Illustrated, March 23, 2009; Wyattresearch.com reports that 78% of NFL players and 60% of NBA players file for bankruptcy within five years of retirement

Lifetime Earnings for Professional Athletes

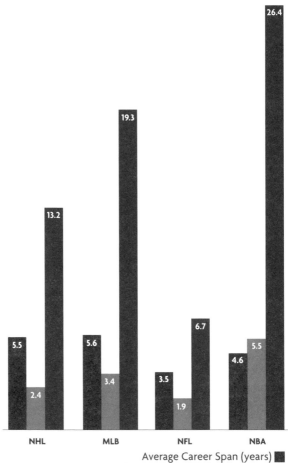

Why So Many Athletes Are Going Broke, February 26/13, www.businessinsider.com

The likelihood too is that these financial pressures will increase the odds that you will divorce after your playing days are over.

I wrote my book based on my experience in working with pro athletes, not only to alert them to the challenges they'll face during their careers, but also to outline a tried-and-true-strategy, which I call "The Pro's Process," that can help them avoid many of the landmines that have caused so much damage to so many of their fellow players.

How the Book is Organized

Part I draws the connection between the challenges that face pro athletes during their career, and continue to pose a threat in retirement. I also introduce several new challenges to be addressed in retirement.

Part II describes the range of athletes we interviewed, the questions we asked them, and the responses they provided. It also includes a section summarizing the major research conclusions as to what constitute the greatest challenges faced by retiring pro athletes. A major finding is that regardless of the sport, retiring pro athletes all face similar issues.

In Part III we identify some of the key resources currently available to assist players as they transition to life after their sport.

In Part IV, we discuss key differences between a pro athlete's retirement and a more typical retirement. We identify and discuss the Three Periods of Retirement for Pro Athletes, and we outline the key ingredients that identify what we define as a successful career transition.

Chapter 1

The Six Biggest "Landmines" Facing Pro Athletes

Let's take a moment before we move on to remind you of the "Six Biggest Landmines Facing Pro Athletes," because some of them will remain dangers during your retirement.

Why is it that pro athletes get themselves into money trouble with such regularity? Here are the major reasons:

1. Overspending
Simply put, pros think their salaries will go on forever, despite statistics that scream out the opposite. They think it won't end, and that they'll never be able to spend it all. But even earning $2 or $3 million a season, by the time an athlete pays their agent and their taxes, they've got a lot less to spend, and it can go very quickly; especially if the level of spending continues into retirement, even after the paychecks stop.

2. Big Paychecks/Short Career
A pro athlete's money is supposed to outlive his career, but many of them don't "get" that. There's a far shorter period of peak earnings in pro sport than in almost any other profession, and in many cases pro athletes lack the time and/or the desire to understand and monitor their investments.

3. They Just Don't Understand Finances
While several pro leagues are now offering seminars on personal finance for athletes, it's still an issue they don't fully understand, and the information isn't always communicated effectively. Ed Butowsky, a well-known wealth management expert who works with some of the top athletes in the world asks, "Where in their lifetime were they going to learn

anything about money? At no point did they learn about personal finance—what a mutual fund is, how the equity markets work, asset allocation. None of that stuff."

Athletes see prominent business people spending a lot of money, and some feel they should be able to do the same thing. A major difference though, according to an accountant who works with many pro athletes, is that "businesspeople spend their lives studying and working with money, while athletes spend their lives studying, training for, and playing their sports."

4. Poor Investment Choices

Young, wealthy and financially illiterate people are prime targets for those selling "can't miss" investments such as nightclubs, restaurants, casino developments, real estate ventures, and other private equity-type deals.

Chronic over-allocation into real estate and bad private equity deals is the #1 problem in terms of financial melt-downs" for pro athletes.

Butowsky says, "Chronic over-allocation into real estate and bad private equity deals is the #1 problem in terms of financial meltdowns" for pro athletes; overspending is #2. According to him, only 1 in 30 (that's about 3%) legitimate private investment deals pan out they way they were advertised. And with the outright scams thrown into the mix, the odds against private equity deals being successful are microscopic: in the range of 1% - 2%. And yet, Butkowsky says, many athletes have dumped about 95% of their money into those two investment types, where they should have less than 5% of their money allocated.

5. They Entrust Their Money's Management to The Wrong People

According to the N.F.L. Players Association, more than 78 players collectively lost $42 million between 1999 and 2002 as a result of entrusting their money to bad advisors. In fact, most athletes have no idea what's going on with their money. Often, bills are paid by a third party, and none of the financial statements go to the athletes. That's a recipe for disaster. We've heard of the plight of former NHLers Derek Sanderson, Michael Peca, and Darren McCarty, and the more recent action by Jack Johnson who was forced to declare bankruptcy in 2014, despite having earned $18 million (US) over a nine-year career up to the 2014-15 campaign, and being on track to earn $5 million per season through 2017-18!

6. Gambling/ Trouble with The Tax Man/ Alimony Payments/ Excessive Leverage

This final grouping is the result of an almost predictable downward spiral, precipitated by the athlete's failure to avoid the "landmines" described above. Desperation leads to an attempt to recover losses through gambling, often with borrowed money. Taxes unpaid during the "glory days" lead to investigation and action by the taxman. Financial stress leads to marital stress and breakdown, which in turn leads to alimony payments. Missed alimony payments lead to legal complications and costs, and situations can spin completely out of control in short order.

No doubt you understand that these risks don't end with retirement.

The press is full of reports (and in *The Pro's Process* we detailed some of the stories) of athletes who "had it all" and then through a combination of the factors outlined above, simply blew it...often to the tune of several million dollars. In the NFL, several high profile players including Warren Sapp, Vince Young, and Rocket Ismail have lost big money. In the NBA, we know that Alan "The Answer" Iverson and Antoine Walker, to name two, have experienced financial turmoil and loss. And of course there are the sad stories of boxers Evander Holyfield and Mike Tyson.

Consider this:

The average employee in the U.S. will work 35-40 years, earning lifetime income of $1.5 to $3 million. Most will enjoy peak earnings in the five years preceding retirement.

The average pro athlete will play for 7-17 years (depending on the sport), and earn between $5 million and $25 million, 70%-90% of which will be earned before age 35.

FIBA Athletes Financial Handbook 2009

The Six Biggest "Landmines" Facing Pro Athletes

I wrote this book so that when the time comes to "hang 'em up," you'll be well equipped to handle the challenges you'll inevitably face as you transition from your pro career to the rest of your life. Some of those challenges will be extensions of the ones you faced during your playing career, such as the continued complexity of your financial situation, post-retirement and secondary career decisions and training, and being the target of cyber fraud or identity theft. But others will be entirely new in retirement, such as the increased likelihood of experiencing serious financial pressure, a greater likelihood of divorce, going from a highly regimented lifestyle to being at "loose ends," and the psychological trauma you'll inevitably experience as you move through the Three Periods of Retirement.

Chapter 2

Who We Interviewed and What We Asked

Over the course of eight months in 2015, we conducted dozens of interviews with retired professional athletes (mostly former NHL players) and their spouses.

Among the interviewees were:
- Canadians, Americans, and Europeans.
- Players who attended U.S. colleges.
- Players who developed through more traditional junior hockey ranks.
- Players who played in the NHL, AHL and ECHL.
- Players who played in Europe.
- Players who appeared in fewer than 100 NHL games.
- Players who played more than 1,000 NHL games.
- Players who retired recently.
- Players who have been retired for a decade or more.
- Players with career earnings that ranged from less than $1 million to nearly $50 million.
- Stanley Cup winners.
- World Hockey Championship winners.
- Olympic medal winners.
- A Grey Cup winner and CFL All-Star.
- Players whose careers ended through injury.
- Players who decided when it was their time to retire.
- Coaches and assistant coaches.

In total, nearly 250 years of professional athletic experience is represented in our interviews.

In addition to conducting interviews, we reviewed literature on the topic that's available in North America (mostly related to the NFL and NBA), in the U.K. (mostly related to football/

Who We Interviewed and What We Asked

soccer and rugby), and in Australia (mostly related to tennis and cricket). We also read transcripts and listened to audio recordings with dozens of players who were interviewed on the topic. We were unable to locate any research related to the impact of a pro athlete's retirement on a spouse and family from the perspective of a spouse, so we made a special effort to speak to players' spouses and significant others.

What We Asked
Our questions were grouped under the following general headings:
- What players miss most about their careers.
- The aspects of the transition they found most difficult.
- The aspects of the transition they found easiest.
- The extent to which they planned for retirement while still playing.
- The advice they received from mentors, coaches, and colleagues about planning for life after retirement from the game.
- The extent to which they felt a "hole" (loss, depression, sadness, a "flat" feeling) in their lives upon retirement, and how they addressed it.
- The impact of retirement on their marriage; if and how their spouse assisted in the transition.
- Advice they'd offer other players nearing retirement.
- Their recommendations on what resources should be available to assist players in the transition.

(Both player and spouse questionnaires are included in the Appendix.)

Chapter 3

What Do You Miss Most About Your Playing Career?

The most common response to this question was one word: "camaraderie." And every single player we interviewed used it. Other phrases included the lack of a regular routine in retirement, the lack of an imposed schedule, the atmosphere of the dressing room, "being with the guys," the intensity of competition, the extremely high level of competition, striving for a common goal, the sense of teammates becoming family, and the passion associated with the game itself. One player confessed that when he retired, he missed the team more than he missed the game. Others missed being in elite physical shape, the end of a period of being well paid for doing something they loved to do, or the loss of a striving environment that was dedicated to the pursuit of a high-level goal.

Others commented that when their career was over, they no longer felt comfortable in the room; they felt left out while others continued their careers, despite the friendships they'd made in the room. One player mentioned the loss of the adrenaline rush that comes when stepping on the ice before the game, with the lights flashing and the crowd cheering. Another said that he continues to miss the routine of training, practicing, and playing...13 years after retiring.

"It's hard to replace the passion you have for a sport. There aren't many jobs that you retire from where you get to prove that you are the very best of the best in front of thousands and thousands of people every night."
—Al Iafrate, NHL player with the hardest slap shot ever recorded.

Those who seemed happiest in their next careers were those who were able in some way, to recreate that sense of camaraderie and team. Russ Courtnall found it in the real estate business: "I'm back to the hockey life. I've got teammates, co-workers, and a boss. I love it!" Other players have found it by becoming fire-fighters or paramedics, enjoying that tight-knit world complete with its emphasis on teamwork, work ethic, regimented schedule, and physical fitness.

There was absolutely no doubt from our conversations, that the single thing they miss most was the camaraderie associated with the team, the game, and striving for the ultimate goal of winning the Stanley Cup.

Chapter 4

What Were the Hardest Parts of Retirement?

Before discussing the biggest challenges retiring players face, a couple of contextual comments are in order. First, not one athlete we interviewed looked eagerly forward to the end of his career; quite the opposite. Without exception, deep down, every athlete we interviewed wished their careers could have gone on longer, even those who retired on their own terms.

"As an athlete, retiring is the toughest decision you have to make, and I didn't make it lightly...It goes against every grain in my body to consider a future without the game. But after 15 years the toll on my body has finally caught up with me."
—Retired MLB player Michael Cuddyer, as quoted in The Players Tribune, December 12, 2015. This quote echoes the feelings of nearly every pro athlete in every major sport.

Second, the challenges confronting retiring players were experienced most acutely by those who left the game entirely. Players who remained in the game in some capacity, whether in coaching, scouting, or management were able to avoid some of them, presumably by the very fact that they remained in the environment and culture they loved so much. (Some research suggests that players may attempt to remain in the game in some capacity, in part because they doubt their ability to apply their experience and character strengths to other careers. Clearly though, there are very few opportunities to remain in the game as compared to the number of players who retire every year.)

"This transition has challenged me financially, emotionally, socially, intellectually, physically and spiritually. I freely admit that I struggled with it for a while, and truth be told, even after twelve years, I still do from time to time."
—Don Davey, a nine-year NFL veteran, who was forced to retire due to a knee injury.

The Seven Biggest Challenges in Retirement
Seven themes emerged from our conversations on the topic. While we highlight only one or two players under each heading here, the seven challenges were identified in multiple interviews.

1. The loss of routine.
Somewhat surprisingly, this challenge was among the most difficult to address for a large number of the players we spoke to. Cory Cross said his time was heavily regimented by others during his playing career, and that in retirement, it was entirely up to him to decide how to allocate it. As he put it, "The discipline that made me successful in the game had to be transferred to life." Pavel Kubina recounted how on game days during his lengthy career, his time was entirely regimented from 9 am to 11 pm. Suddenly, in retirement, it was entirely up to him. For months, Pavel felt "out of sorts" as he transitioned from having almost no control over his life to having total control. It was a difficult transition, to say the least.

Sean O'Donnell said he missed the routine most, and found it very difficult to adjust. "When the routine controls your life, winter and summer, for 20 years and then it's over...I know it sounds silly, but having to make simple decisions like what to eat for lunch...it can be a tough adjustment." But then, just three months later, his daughter was born and he was forced into a new routine that had nothing to do with him and everything to do with the baby. He says it diverted his attention from what he was missing and focused it on a new, more important routine.

2. Filling the "hole" in your life.
Wade Redden described it this way: "In the game, there's in-tensity, focus, dedication and passion. When it's over and all the intensity and passion is gone, there's a hole in your life." He recounts how he and his wife Danica had young children at that time, and how their activities and needs created a very busy life, which filled the hole to some degree. He also commented that he hasn't yet found a new passion or focus that provides the same intensity his career did. As a result, the hole hasn't yet been completely filled for him.

Another player commented that the the hole seems deeper when you're wondering, "What will I do now?" while other people's lives seem to roll smoothly along.

3. No more big paychecks.
Shaun Van Allen shared the "frightening" feeling of being one year into retirement, having no money coming in, and being at home with their young special-needs child while his wife, a pharmacist, was at work. He said you make good money

as an NHL player, but if you're not a superstar, "You know you're not set for life. When there's no consistent paycheck, you don't really know what you want to do, and you're just working to survive, it's tough." Especially, he added, when you pretty

A player who leaves the game in his 30s faces the daunting prospect of 60+ years of inflation continuously eroding the value of his investments. In dollar terms, this means a $250,000 per year lifestyle today will be the equivalent of a $750,000 per year lifestyle thirty years from now.

much know for sure that you'll never find anything that earns the level of income you enjoyed while playing. He acknowledges his wife's profession for helping get them through that rough patch; "I don't know where we'd be if she didn't have her education." Subsequently, Shaun landed a coaching job at Carleton University and now finds time to coach his son's hockey team and to do charity work with the Ottawa Senators.

A player who leaves the game in his 30s faces the daunting prospect of 60+ years of inflation continuously eroding the value of his investments. In dollar terms, this means a $250,000 per year lifestyle today will be the equivalent of a $750,000 per year lifestyle thirty years from now.

Chris Kontos told a similar story. While he found work covering sports for a local television station shortly after retirement, he was coping with life on a much lower salary than he'd earned while playing for the Los Angeles Kings. As a result, he and his family were forced to make significant adjustments to their spending habits and lifestyle. He was able to do it, but there are many examples of players who—despite earning a much lower income—refuse to make the necessary spending changes. The next stop for them is bankruptcy.

When I did go on vacation, I'd fly in economy class to harden myself for the real world. I once flew 20 hours to New Zealand in coach, even though my salary was millions of dollars a year (because as I've explained before, NHL players only take home a fraction of that). Sure, people would say, "Hey, look, Sean Avery is flying coach!"...but the thing many players fail to realize when they leave the game is that they've been living in a world that's only possible if you're fabulously wealthy. All the private jets, the five-star hotels, the catered gourmet meals, the freebies in bars and restaurants, plus the crazy money for playing a game can make you forget that you're really a guy from suburban Ontario and your parents are teachers. Sure, flying 20 hours in coach sucks. But you need to remember that you're a normal human being before it's too late. It's not just about the money. It's about keeping your expectations in check.

—Sean Avery

The Boston Globe reported in 2014 that as many as 100 former NHL players, coaches, trainers, and widows receive assistance from the NHL Players Association emergency fund at any given time; totaling about $2 million per year.

Former Chicago Blackhawk Steve Ludzik says he knows of many former NHL players who live hand to mouth. "I know guys who you once were cheering for on Saturday nights who are now looking for something to eat. I know guys who are living in trailer homes or tents." His charity Players Helping Players commits money raised from player appearances and signing events to help former NHL players who have fallen on hard times. Ludzik is currently negotiating with developers in the Niagara Falls area to build a retirement home in Chippewa, Ontario that might accommodate up to 50 former NHL players who need a place to stay.

4. Being *forced* to retire really sucks!
It's bad enough for a player when he comes to the realization that it's time to move on from the game. It's worse when that decision is taken out of your hands as the result of a career-ending injury at a young age.

Grant Clitsome found himself in that unenviable position in 2015 at the age of just 30. The biggest challenge, he confessed, was accepting that it was over; somehow being OK with it, keeping up his spirits and trying to be "pleasant to be around," even when he didn't feel pleasant. For Grant and other players who face a similar fate, the feeling that such a big part of their lives has been simply ripped away is very difficult to process. Grant reminisced about missing training camp when others were headed back, missing the familiar routine, missing being around the guys and the locker room. At the same time, he was forced to consider (much earlier than he ever anticipated) what he was going to do and to find a new purpose that would inspire him in the next phase of his life.

When we spoke to him in September of 2015, he was just back from consulting with his back surgeon who informed him his career was over, and from visiting his team mates to tell them the same news—a trip that must have been a very difficult one to make. But he made a comment suggesting that he'd be able to move on. He said, "I'm trying to be thankful for what I had—the relationships, the travel, the pride in the achievements, and opportunities I was given—rather than regretful over the losses."

Todd White was also forced from the game by injury. In his case, it ended when he suffered his seventh concussion, a blow delivered accidently by a teammate. It caused excruciating headaches that he hadn't experienced as a result of any previous concussion. He found it difficult to come to grips with the fact that he was not going to win a Stanley Cup, feeling that he had a chance at that prize had he been able to play a little longer. When retirement was forced on him sooner than anticipated, he also felt the acute loss of his long-time routine; he floundered with a lack of regimented schedule for his days. He was also forced to consider what he'd do in retirement at an earlier date than he'd anticipated (not that he'd given it much thought before that time). He feared jumping into a post-playing venture too quickly, not just in case he wasn't successful at it, but also because he feared disappointing someone who'd given him the opportunity in the first place. Over and over again in our interviews, we heard examples of this loss of personal confidence expressed by world-class athletes who, to all outside appearances, were completely self-assured.

5. Too many options can make the "right" decision difficult. Tyler Sloan started to think a little about retirement when he was about 25 years of age. He learned about the Career Enhancement Program, which is managed by the Professional Hockey Players Association (to which players in the American Hockey League and East Coast Hockey League belong), and some of the options he could pursue in preparing for life after hockey. But like many players we spoke to, he opted to maintain his focus on doing all he could to perform at the highest level possible in order to extend his career for as long as he could.

As his career wound down though, he wasn't being given as much playing time as he felt he deserved, he began to feel frustrated at the way things were going, and so began to more seriously consider the options available to him.

He thought of going to play in Europe, thinking he could continue his career and at the same time travel and sightsee, and in retrospect, regrets not doing that. It was his advice that players should stay in the game as long as they have a contribution, and get it completely out of their system before they retire. On the other hand, he decided that it would be more difficult to come back from Europe at age 38 and try to find something, than it would be to start the search at age 32.

A short time later, as his heart was telling him that his hockey days were coming to an end, and as he was seeking advice from other players who'd gone through the transition, he was presented with a sales opportunity in the oil and gas industry in Alberta. He thought it would give him an opportunity to gain some business experience, to grow his network, and to replace his lost hockey routine with a new one, one that could give his life renewed focus.

He accepted the job, but he hated it, and found the year he spent at the job to be very difficult. He began to question his own decision-making abilities; he knew this job wasn't for him long-term, but didn't know what job was. The situation scared him, and he experienced severe mood swings. When we spoke to Tyler, he told us about several other players he knew of who experienced similar feelings as they tried to get their feet under them after hockey.

After leaving the sales job, Tyler sought career counseling, investigated several other options, and ultimately decided to purchase a safety supply company that provides products and services in the oil and gas sector. He's feeling much happier, more optimistic and "nicer to be around these days," and says he feels he's "getting a business degree on the job." When we asked him how he turned things around, he replied that he forced himself to take the "scary step," to try things, to be proactive, and to embrace the fact that he'll likely have two or three more careers before he's finished—so he simply forced himself to get on with it.

"We gain little to no training in marketing, accounting, finance, sales, management, technology or any other key element required for a company to be successful. One former player was told by a potential employer, *'To put it bluntly, you have no transferrable skills.'* Take full advantage of the networking opportunities the league affords you while you're playing, but manage your expectations. The truth is most of us will likely need to learn to provide for ourselves."
—Don Davey

6. "I quit playing too soon."
Grant Carter's biggest challenge in leaving pro football was that he quickly became convinced he left it too soon. Seeing former teammates and college friends staying on and continuing to thrive in the game he loved and left (by choice), left a lasting sense of regret in Grant. For him, the "hole" in his life was caused by a sense of lost opportunity or the belief (after the fact) that he'd made a poor decision about the timing of his retirement. That, in turn, created an emotional challenge that he associated with the loss of camaraderie, which so many athletes feel so deeply. His feelings were further exacerbated by being forced to come to grips with the fact that he'd seriously underestimated the realities and difficulties associated with the transition to civilian life. He says he endured three to four years of internal struggle or tug-of-war over his decision to retire. "It diminishes over time." He says, but still—having been retired for 14 years—he feels he left too soon.

"I sympathize with guys that retire that are not at peace with it. The problem is most guys never set themselves up to do something (different), and I found it very depressing for a lot of guys."
—Former Detroit Pistons star Chauncey Billups, a five-time NBA All-Star

Marc Chorney tells a similar story. While he too retired from the NHL on his own terms, he nonetheless felt great loss at the fact that he was no longer doing what he'd been trained to do for much of his life. He too saw former pro and college teammates continue their careers after his retirement, and he felt that had circumstances been different, he too could have contributed at the NHL level for another five years. He voices that regret to this day, though he retired from the game 30 years ago.

For Marc's wife Lynn, the most difficult part of Marc's retirement was the loss of the friendships she'd developed with other wives. Players lose the camaraderie with their teammates; their spouses lose a similar camaraderie with other players' wives. These wives supported each other during times when their husbands struggled with injury, or being traded, or being benched, or being sent down to the minors. She commented that the game can be "brutal" to players and their families, and feels that the life of a pro player is overly romanticized. Pros have so little control over their lives, and the friendships Lynn developed while Marc was playing served as a safety net against the uncertainties that are so much a part of a player's hockey life. When Marc retired, this important part of Lynn's life ended too.

7. Venturing outside their comfort zone.
Several players we interviewed were challenged by being
forced to think, for the first time ever in a serious way, about
what they'd do after their careers were finished. Others
struggled with a wide range of options, but seemingly lacked
the self-confidence to decide which way to go.

Cory Cross faced a different challenge: he'd experienced a
lockout during his career. While the season was on hold, he
studied for his real estate license and subsequently sold
a few properties. At the same time, he was aware that his
career was winding down, so he began actively searching for
other post-hockey opportunities.

Discussions with his agent led him to invest in an oil and gas
service company while he finished the last year of his career
playing in Europe. During that year, he decided the time had
come where (unlike many other players we interviewed who
regretted leaving the game too soon), "The company needed
me more than I needed hockey." So he retired and dove in
to the new business—one in which he had no background
or experience. And while there were times of severe stress
in the transition, Cory was grateful that he had a place to go
after hockey, unlike many who drift for a time. The biggest
challenge for him wasn't deciding what to do after hockey;
rather it was, "How am I going to learn all I need to know
about this new business as fast as possible?" He found the
learning curve very steep, and admits that at first, he thought
he knew a bit about how business works. But before long he

realized just how complex the new business was, and was grateful to have partners who were more experienced who taught him the ropes. Like other players who moved into business, Cory reports, "I felt I got a business degree without going to school."

Part of the role Cory took on in the business initially involved significant travel. His wife Shannon remembered that in the early days of his new business, he hit the ground running, and was actually away more than he was while playing in the NHL. But, she said, while many of his retired hockey friends were bored and let their fitness level decline in retirement, Cory was never bored, and he didn't allow his fitness level to suffer. On the other hand, she said, he was so busy he didn't go to the rink for a year after retirement.

For her part, Shannon reported feeling some of the same the loss of camaraderie she enjoyed with other player wives as Lynn Chorney did. She too said she became used to the "perks" and the lifestyle that came with being married to an NHL player, and found it difficult to transition to a more normal life when it was over.

An Exception to the "Rule."
It's said in research that there's an exception to every rule and that often, the exception proves the rule.

The exception in this study is exemplified by Mike Foligno: a 15-year, 1,000+ game NHL veteran, and father of two current NHLers, Nick and Marcus.

Mike reported that he lost contact with many former

teammates after he retired, but that he did not find the loss as debilitating as others have reported. Unlike many players who report feelings of depression or ennui after leaving the game, Mike says the reason for it, he believes, is that he was ready. He was satisfied that he always gave his very best, and had no regrets about his career at all. So when he was no longer able to train at the level he expected of himself, rather than going to play a few more years in Europe, he decided that he would either compete at the highest level or not at all.

At the same time, he looked forward to being able to spend more time with his boys, who were developing their own hockey skills, and who kept a hectic schedule of activities. He loved the family-oriented activities such as taking the boys to early morning practice and then going for breakfast; he also relished being able to finally attend their school activities.

So while he admits that he had an easier time deciding to call it a career than many players we spoke too, he did experience that "hole" in his life for a while. For a time, he filled it by investing in a start-up company that manufactured goal nets for street hockey made of PVC plastic, instead of the traditional and much heavier metal. It's also true that he had the opportunity to become involved in the game again about a year after retirement, when he was offered a coaching job with the Toronto Maple Leafs, though he'd retired initially without that prospect on the horizon.

Biggest Challenges According to the Research

In this section, I've extracted concepts and key information from a variety of research reports published in North America and beyond. I've tried to keep the information practical and useful by offering a commentary on the sources, rather than quoting them chapter and verse, and citing every individual source. The sources consulted are listed in the Bibliography in the Appendix.

- One study identified five key challenges faced by retiring pro and elite athletes.

They include:

1. *Denial*—not being able to face the reality that the game is over, that your life will be different.
2. *Increased drinking and drug use*—often an existing problem that becomes bigger in retirement.
3. *Divorce*—it's reported that HALF of NFL players get divorced within the first year of retirement.
4. *Depression*—very few seek or are provided with mental health therapy during their transition.
5. *Isolation*—anger, bitterness, lack of structure, and financial stress may increase this feeling.

- There's a physical, psychological and emotional disengagement from being a pro or elite athlete that no one is effectively addressing.

- People who fall in love with the game get heartbroken because the game doesn't have a heart, or the ability to

love them back. By falling in love with it, they set themselves up for disappointment and struggles, especially
in the early days of retirement.

- Pro athletes face the same emotional and financial
  challenges that the average Joe faces. The difference is
  that pro athletes face them at a much earlier stage of life
  than others—often at a time when they're not as mature
  or capable of handling them as those who retire later
  in life.

- Because athletes spend much of their time dedicated
  to their sport at an early age, this creates a situation in
  which time has not been allocated to acquiring interests in other areas. As a result, athletes often identify
  exclusively with the role of athlete. Consequently, when
  they retire from their sport, they may feel acute loss and
  become disillusioned.

- Athletes often fail to give credit to the lessons and skills
  acquired through their sporting career. This may result in
  tunnel vision, where they're unable to see how the same
  skills that made them successful in their sport will make
  them successful in other career pathways.

- Athletes may not be prepared for the transition into
  athletic retirement because they've become dependent
  on others for such factors as personal management.
  They have little voice in their training or competition,
  and thus can become overly dependent on coaches for
  decision-making.

- In addition to the loss of old support systems, they may not have the ability to quickly create a new support system; this can lead to feelings of isolation.

- Athletes who retire involuntarily (through injury) are often more resistant and less well-prepared emotionally than those who retire voluntarily.

- Some athletes believe they are "nothing" without their sports and that their skills are useless if they're no longer involved in sport. Other athletes expect to be immediately successful at a career outside their sport.

- Still others become overly focused on the negative aspects of their transition, and forget to include the positive aspects. All three of these approaches add to the already significant challenges they face in the transition.

Chapter 5

What Were the Easiest Parts of Retirement?

• A more normal family life.
After a lifetime of following a highly regimented routine, many players and spouses appreciated the opportunity for a more normal family life, and the luxury of controlling their own time.

Players appreciated the chance to attend and coach kids' hockey games, to attend school plays, and to support children who were involved in other sports and activities. Wives appreciated the support that their husbands could now provide in driving kids to practices, to recitals, to games, and school activities after years when they did it pretty much on their own, while players were away on road trips, at games, or at practice.

• Didn't miss the intense training and the constant aches and pains.
Almost every player mentioned how much they appreciated the respite from the constant banging and the nagging injuries that are part and parcel of a pro athlete's life, at least during the season. At the same time, many mentioned how much they enjoyed the training aspect of their careers, and intended to continue to keep themselves in the best physical shape possible.

• Knowing they were immediately moving on to an exciting new challenge.

"The quicker you find a new passion the better. The longer it takes, the greater the likelihood of deeper and deeper problems." —A 20-year NHL veteran.

Those players and spouses who looked forward to immediately beginning an exciting new chapter in their lives, even though success was by no means guaranteed, found the transition easier than those who were uncertain about their futures. The new challenge immediately created a new routine to replace the one they were used to, easing their anxieties and uncertainties about the future. It certainly prevented the boredom we found in some athletes who hadn't yet found a focus for the next part of their lives.

For some, the new challenge was in the form of a business venture; for others, it involved television or radio work connected with the game; for yet others, it involved charitable work on behalf of their former team.

• Fewer game-related insecurities.
Sean O'Donnell expressed this idea very powerfully, and echoed the comments of others when he said that he didn't for a minute miss the constant insecurity that's a part of the life of a pro athlete. He said it comes from a fear of being benched for a bad shift, being sat out of a game despite the fact that you're not injured (a "healthy scratch"), the fear of being sent down to the minors, or the fear that a strained relationship with the coach could lead to any of the above. He said it's constant, and it's pervasive, and it can impact your entire season or career.

All of these insecurities are magically lifted, he said, the moment you announce your retirement.

While these insecurities will no doubt be replaced by others as part of the player's transition to life after the game, for the moment, it can feel like a huge weight has been lifted from one's shoulders.

"I didn't love the constant uncertainty that my career could end at any moment. It's difficult to explain to a fan, but your life as a professional athlete is colored by uncertainty. You worry about making a bad play, taking a bad penalty, missing a golden opportunity to score a goal. The pressure that we experience while we're playing can be depressing. You know you're one small piece of a large machine, and there are guys in suits in the stands watching how you help or hurt that machine. They have pressures on them too, and some general manager can panic about his own job, and suddenly you get a phone call saying, 'You've been traded to another team.' It's part of the job but it's never normal."
—11-year NHL veteran Sean Avery on why he decided to retire in 2012.

• Retirement is made easier by the presence of a group of
  friends unconnected to the game.
Several players commented on this phenomenon. It's probably due to the fact that by having friends who are unrelated to the game, it's easier to fit into a new social routine. It also fills the void that many players referred to, created when the camaraderie of the dressing room comes to an end at retirement. In effect, a player with friends outside the game has an ongoing camaraderie with them, which helps buffer the loss felt by those who have no "replacement" buddies. Steve

Montador, who experienced severe difficulties in his transition, often commented that as difficult a time as he was having, it was made easier by a group of friends who helped him as best they could.

• A college degree provided "options" and a sense of confidence. Just 10 years ago, only 20% of NHL players came with a college background. Growth since then has been remarkable to the point that in the 2013-14 season, 305 former college players skated in the NHL—31% of players in the league. While we don't know how many of them earned their degree, 92% of NCAA Men's Hockey players graduate; that's #1 among all men's sports.[1] The NCAA now refers to itself as The Logical Path to The NHL.

"Let's be realistic. At 16 years old, how many kids are actually going to make it to the NHL? I wanted a fallback plan. I didn't want to put all my eggs in one basket, so I thought I'd go to school and get an education. If I could make it to the NHL out of college, great, and if not I had a (finance) degree to fall back on."
—Kevin Bieksa/Bowling Green.[1]

That's exactly the message we heard from the college players we spoke to who made it to the NHL...a college degree provides options.

But according to some of our interviewees, it goes beyond actually completing the degree. Some of them said that even when the specifics of their degree weren't critical to success (such as it might in accounting or finance), the fact that

1. College Hockey Inc.com; Oct 28/14

they'd been able to meet the demanding academic requirements of a four-year degree gave them the confidence to
believe they could handle almost any challenge that came
their way. Despite his career-ending back injuries, Grant
Clitsome knows that with his degree in entrepreneurship
and business, he has options.

And as University of Maine head hockey coach Dennis
Gendron noted, "This generation of players I'm coaching now,
many of them will live into their 100s. If you're lucky, you'll
play professional hockey until you're 40. You still have six-
tenths of your life to live."

**"Some players don't have the confidence that they
can do something well after hockey. My husband went
to college, and while it's no guarantee of a job after
hockey, it was important because it gave him the confidence that he could successfully do something after
hockey. He knew he had options."**
—A hockey wife.

Chris Kontos reported on a hopeful and positive change of
attitude taking place within the sport. When his son, who
was playing in Orlando in the ECHL, decided to accept a
hockey scholarship at St. Francis Xavier, his Orlando coaches
were supportive of his decision and assured him that he'd
be welcome back there after his schooling if he wished
to return. It seems as well that NHL scouts are increasing-
ly looking to the college ranks in Canada and the U.S. as
sources of NHL talent.

Having said that, there's no denying the fact that degree or not, as Todd White put it: "There's nothing easy about it when your life-long dream's been taken away."

Chapter 6

To What Extent Did You Prepare for Retirement While Still Playing?

The majority of respondents agreed that while playing, it was "all hockey, all the time" in order to remain at the top of their game. In so doing, they would extend their careers as long as possible.

Pavel Kubina felt that it was simply impossible for guys who were thinking of business ventures while they played, or what they'd do in their next careers, to remain at the top of their game.

Shaun Van Allen said that the idea of preparing for retirement while still playing created a dilemma for him. "To be at the top of your game, you need to focus on it," he said. "If you begin to think about life after, it can take away your focus and become a self-fulfilling prophecy. No one wants to do anything to detract from playing at the highest level possible." So Shaun limited his post-hockey career planning to a decision to leave the game with no debt.

As Sean O'Donnell neared the age of 35 and the end of his career, he began to contemplate next steps, but "As a player, I was all in, focused on the next practice or the next game, and everything else faded away."

Dave Farrish gave very little consideration to the "after," until near the end of his career when he decided that he wanted to remain in the game, if he could, as a coach. Neither did Tyler Sloan, who didn't know what he wanted to do after hockey, and therefore remained focused on playing at the highest possible level, and remaining in the game as long as he could. His observation was that like him, lots of guys didn't want to think at all about what might happen after their pro careers.

Mike Foligno became involved in the early days of the growth of the health and fitness club industry while still a player. But he found it very complicated and draining when he had to make decisions about paying rent for their facility, the purchase and lease of equipment, marketing, budgeting, and all the other aspects of running a business. So he sold out early, before the boom in the industry took hold. The lesson he learned was that, for him, a business venture was a distraction from a necessary focus on his hockey performance; he vowed there'd be no more of that during his career and determined to do whatever he did at 100%.

Grant Carter thought about life after football during the off season, and even more as he neared the end of his career and realized it wasn't a question of "if" he'd be done, but rather "when." So when he saw others leaving the game and going to "nothing," losing confidence and losing families, he was determined to be proactive and to seek out opportunities that appealed to him, even though he could have played longer.

But several of the players we talked to responded differently to the question. They felt it was possible and important to begin pre-planning possible post-career activities. We've referred to Cory Cross who not only earned his real estate license during a lockout, but also invested in an oil and gas supply firm while still playing, although he wasn't involved in its day-to-day management while he was still playing. Russ Courtnall had an early interest in real estate, at the age of 22 he earned his license, just in case his hockey career didn't develop.

Wade Redden focused attention on his game, but fairly early in his playing career invested in a business operated by a friend. Now in retirement, he's involved in it to a greater degree.

Several players who came to the NHL via the college route, including Marc Chorney and Todd White, said that the fact that they decided to go to college before playing in the NHL indicated their commitment to looking forward to their post-hockey lives. Grant Carter also saw his decision to attend college before playing pro as a long-term planning decision.

"I started to plan my escape route. I opened my first bar, Warren 77, in 2009, while I was playing for the Rangers, and I began talking to an advertising guy about joining his firm when I left the game. A lot of people laughed at me when I took an internship at Vogue during the offseason. I schlepped clothes to photo shoots and picked up catering from 9-to-5. But I also got to see how some of the brightest minds in fashion worked and it gave me some legitimate work experience to take into my first real job."
—Sean Avery

Grant Clitsome took the pre-planning one step further by studying for the GMAT (Graduate Management Admission Test). It's the standardized test commonly used by business schools to assess the readiness of applicants for an MBA program. However, before the examination date, he was called up to the NHL where he finished his career. During his playing career, Grant acquired an interest in learning more about wine, so he enrolled in several wine courses and completed the Wine & Spirits Education Trust (WSET) accreditation, which is generally regarded as one of the world's leading providers of wine education.

The late Steve Montador also attempted to prepare for a post-hockey career by enrolling at the University of Phoenix, which provides many on-line courses. Like many players though, he found that while there's considerable discussion about the "down time" that athletes have at their disposal, and how they could use that time more productively, the reality didn't always coincide with the theory. Steve found that there were often last minute changes made by the team to a player's schedule, and that as a result, the hour or so he might have arranged for a group Skype discussion with other students or faculty would have to be postponed or cancelled.

The determination required by players to complete such courses or programs during the season is monumental, and sometimes made more difficult by a sense that the team is not always supportive of such player activity—feeling it may detract from their on-ice performance.

Fortunately, it appears as if this anti-preparation sentiment is gradually giving way to a more enlightened approach. By researching how sporting organizations in other countries prepared their athletes for retirement—England, Australia, and New Zealand provided data on soccer, rugby and cricket teams, as well as tennis players—we learned that many of the athletes who took part in retirement preparation actually saw an uptick in their on-field performance, not the opposite, as we've always assumed here in North America. Perhaps before long, more coaches in North America will come to understand that those athletes who maintain a healthy balance in their lives are those most likely to excel in their chosen sport.

Chapter 7

What Advice Did You Receive from Others?

Based on the answers discussed above, relatively little retirement advice or counsel is given to players by other players. The reason, it seems, is that most of them have given relatively little thought to it themselves, and no-one really knows exactly what to expect when they leave the game. Therefore, it's difficult to know what to say to others who might ask, and relatively few players seem to want to ask (or to know) what to expect in the first place. They seem to prefer to live in the "here and now," giving their all to the game, and frankly, living in something of a fool's paradise.

Here are some other observations and tidbits of advice offered by retired players:

- "Be nice to people on the way up, because you're going to see them again on the way down."

- "Don't think too much about it now, or you'll lose your edge."

- When they played together in Toronto, Borje Salming offered the following suggestion to Russ Courtnall: "Be yourself and be humble. Playing the game is only what you do...it's not who you are. You are more than a hockey player; you are a human being. We have been blessed to play this game at the highest level, but there is more to us than that."

- "It didn't matter what anybody said, I wasn't listening. I was 23 years old; I thought I was Superman, that I'd play forever, and that I'd earn a boatload of money."

What Advice Did You Receive from Others?

- Tyler Sloan spent most of his career in the AHL, with comparatively low lifetime earnings of about $1.3 million, and he knew he'd have to find other work. So he actively asked for advice from others both inside and outside hockey, and he shared some of it with us:

  ◇ Try anything and everything; get a job anywhere to gain experience; look for internships; "shadow" people whose jobs interest you.
  ◇ Follow your interests.
  ◇ Stay busy, be proactive. Don't wait for phone calls, make phone calls instead.
  ◇ Create a new routine to replace your former one; you need a routine or you'll stagnate.
  ◇ Talk to people; network; go to charity events; "A lot of it's who you know."
  ◇ Join the Alumni (in his case the Calgary Flames chapter).

- Mike Foligno told us that years ago, teammate Red Berenson advised him to buy more units of the Players' Pension Fund. Mike says, "At the time, I remember thinking, 'What's a pension?' I was 21 years old and couldn't have cared less about pensions. But Red's advice was good and I should have listened to him."

- Sean O'Donnell said, "You must be fearless on the ice, even if you feel scared; but reaching out to a psychologist or counselor or an advisor for help (as you transition to retirement) is not a sign of weakness. It's a sign of intelligence and strength."

Chapter 8

To What Extent Did You Experience "The Hole"?

Our conversations on this question made one thing very clear: those players who had something specific lined up to go to immediately after their careers ended were much less likely to experience depression, or feelings of sadness or flatness. They were less likely to fall into "the hole" than those players who found themselves at loose ends when their career ended.

We concentrate our attention in this section on some of those who did experience "the hole" and who were prepared to share their stories with us.

Dave Farrish commented both from his own experience as a player and as a coach, that he's seen a lot of players "stuck" at the end of their careers. Economics dictates that they change their lifestyle, but they're often unable or unwilling to do so in time, and they don't know how to handle it.

Finances suffer, and so do marriages. They may have little formal education and few skills for the job market. That leads to depression, alcoholism, and drug abuse. "I know a lot of players in that situation," he said, "that no one knows or hears about."

Pavel Kubina's experience with "the hole" is typical of many others. Seeing former teammates and colleagues continue playing brought on feelings of loneliness, and wishing he was still playing himself ("I know I could have played longer, and wish I did.").

After a few months of retirement, he began to ask himself, "What am I going to do tomorrow?" The answer scared him—nothing. "I'd get up at 10:00 am and ask myself what I was going to do for the rest of the day," and the answer was that he had nothing to do. Feeling like this made it easy to sit home and drink, but he knew he had to move on. Thanks to the support and encouragement he received from his good friends, Pavel was able to move on to the next phase of his life, combining his passion for performance cars with a business opportunity: he's now a partner in a high-end car dealership in Tampa.

Steve Montador fell into depression partly as a result of his multiple concussions, partly too because he felt he received very little support from the NHLPA as he transitioned out of the game. He needed help, sought help, and found little. "He just didn't know what he wanted to do next," said his friend and former teammate Daniel Carcillo. "He was searching for that. He was searching for a lot of things, as we're all going to do when we move on." He felt discarded and, as Monty's father Paul put it, he "died with a broken heart."

Sean O'Donnell says he found himself in a "trough" for a short but memorable period of time in post-retirement. He described becoming anxious and even obsessive about a situation close to home that suddenly became very import-ant when he was around the house a lot after retiring. He said there were some power lines near his house that had never bothered him before; but now he became convinced that they were obstructing his view. He became obsessed with them, and couldn't get them out of his mind for several weeks. When he was playing, he'd obsess about a bad shift or a bad game; now his mind told him he had to find something else to obsess over.

Todd White was "irritable" for a while after retirement, but isn't certain whether it was because of retirement or because of career-ending concussions. Either way, it was a difficult and stressful period for him. For the better part of his first full year of retirement, the question in his mind wasn't, "What will I do?" but rather, "How am I going to get myself better?" He was advised by doctors not to work out because of the concussions, and found that directive to be a big loss— because he loved to work out. Lack of the sweat-producing activity he loved aggravated his feelings of irritability. And because he didn't have a clear plan as to what he'd do in retirement, or even where he'd live, he and his wife decided to begin by moving back to his hometown of Ottawa, and simply trying to restart their lives.

Making the situation worse, while he was exploring business options and opportunities, he feared making a bad investment decision because of the examples he'd seen and heard of guys who'd made big business investments only to lose a substantial portion of their investment, if not all of it.

A few of our interviewees made interesting observations (in the context of feelings of depression and sadness) concerning the role their faith played in helping them through this challenging period of their lives.

Marc Chorney's wife, Lynn observed that because Marc had a business opportunity in his immediate post-hockey life, he didn't experience the depths of depression that many others did. She admitted that there was a period of adjustment, but nothing severe. Then she commented that she believed Marc's faith helped during the period immediately following his retirement, especially as he questioned whether he'd left the game too early.

Grant Carter made a similar comment in stating that he had to lean on his faith, and draw strength from it after retirement. This was particularly so when he questioned himself about retiring when he did, given that he too feels he could have played longer.

Chapter 9

What Impact Did Retirement Have on Your Marriage?

We often read stories in the press asserting that the likelihood of divorce spikes for pro athletes after retirement, and there are many specific situations where this is documented. We wanted to speak to a number of players and their spouses about their personal situation, and ask how retirement from the sport impacted their marriages. After all, we know that the transition affects not only the player, but also his spouse and his entire family.

We were also interested to know of specific ways in which a player felt his spouse had been helpful, and to compare his view with hers.

Several players describe their lives as changing abruptly from seeing too little of each other during the playing career, to almost seeing too much of each other after retirement. Todd White said, "I was now home more than she'd like, after years of being gone more than she'd like." This is especially so if the player is depressed, or irritable, or worse, because of a career-ending injury. Such a situation can make for very tense times on the home front, especially if small children are involved.

Too much togetherness can lead to bickering about who's doing what around the house, about the reduced level of income, about one spouse continuing to spend the same amount as they did when much more money was coming in, and so on. These are the irritants that, unchecked, contribute to bigger problems that in turn can mushroom out of control, leading to real acrimony and ultimately, divorce.

Some observers commented they knew of situations where couples discovered that as they spent more time together after the player's retirement from the game, they simply weren't compatible, and the marriages ended.

People file for divorce for all kinds of reasons, including extramarital affairs, money, lack of communication, even weight gain. Any of these issues can come to the forefront once a player is at home every day, and if you combine that with the fact that less money is coming in, the situation can get tense. While a player's career is active, his wife may have overlooked his cheating or the fact that he just didn't listen to anything she had to say, but with him at home every day, she may not be willing to let things go.

Meanwhile, as a retired player, he's not going to be working out regularly and could start putting on some pounds, looking less and less each day like the man she married. Combine all of this, and a lot of wives get fed up and file for divorce.[1]

Danica and Wade Redden found that a partial solution to their "too much time together" problem was for each partner to have their own schedule during the day, and to spend family time together at night. Often, during the player's career, the at-home spouse was self-sufficient, and created a personal and child-raising schedule that worked pretty efficiently. But it was disrupted when the player retired and

1. Winning The Money Game: Lessons Learned from The Financial Fouls of Pro Athletes. Adonal Foyle, 2015, Harper Collins Publishers

wanted to help around the house. With each spouse having an out-of-house routine during the day, they each had their own space and their own time, and could look forward to their time together during the evening.

Some examples were also shared where the wife had totally bought into the lifestyle of the highly paid world-class athlete, including travel to exotic places, the best hotels and meals, lavish entertainment and royal treatment wherever they went. And along with this buy-in was the expectation that it would never end. But at some point it always does, and reality reasserts itself. Several players recounted stories of wives who were either unwilling or unable to deal with the new reality in their lives, and simply left their husbands shortly after they retired from their sport.

We were also told of situations of spouses who had "kept the home fires burning" very effectively during the player's career, by managing the children's lives and carrying a burden similar to that of a single parent for many years. Now there was the added stress of being required to take on the additional role of therapist or counselor for their husbands (who were suffering from their own emotional stresses or depression as a result of their retirement), and who, though they were willing to do so, simply could not cope. Tragic examples like these usually ended in divorce too.

Our discussions also made it clear that it was important as a survival technique for the player's wife to help her husband find a new routine as quickly as possible. It might be a business-related routine, but even if it wasn't job-driven, savvy wives seemed to know how important it was to help their husbands establish new routines quickly.

Being a hands-on father, perhaps for the first time, was one quick way players found of getting into a routine: feeding, changing diapers, cleaning up the house; several of them commented on how quickly they forgot their old routine once they were immersed in the reality, intensity, and "never-ending-ness" of raising kids.

Many appreciated the new family focus rather than the old sports focus of their lives, and relished the opportunity to be more involved with their children's activities than had ever been possible before. More than one couple spoke of the deep sense of "blessedness" they felt in this new stage of their lives.

After retirement, people's lives change. When a pro athlete's schedule finally allows him to spend quality time with his wife at home, he's forced to handle day-to-day issues that in the past he's been able to run away from. Whether it's how to deal with the guests coming over for Thanksgiving or why there are messages on the answering machine from some woman, his schedule with the team made it very easy for him to evade discussions around these matters.

Because of the amount of time spent on the road during their playing days, most retired athletes didn't have a clear role in the household—the wife was the chief of the house. Now that he is there, he may want

a larger role, but exactly what that is can be hard to define after all the years that he wasn't really around.[1]

When asked how his spouse helped him with his transition, Todd White said she took the lead in getting the kids settled when they moved back to Ottawa, she helped nurse him back to health after his career-ending concussion, and she shielded him from the problems that brought on severe headaches.

Danica Redden helped Wade in many ways too. She reinforced that he's more than just a hockey player; she gave him family and child-rearing responsibilities that made him feel he was truly contributing to the family and at the same time, helped create a new routine for him. "Everyone needs to feel needed," she said, and she helped him feel needed. She encouraged him to continue his exercise regime, to set daily goals, and to become involved in the operation of the company in which he was an investor. And she helped him see retirement as one life chapter closing and another just beginning, and not as a challenge or a problem.

Marc Chorney says "Lynn was the glue, the rock for our family." She was the one who kick-started their social life when they moved to a new city. Lynn felt her contributions were based mostly on her ability and willingness to adapt to their new financial reality. Marc says she was very frugal with the family's expenditures, and took in children for day care

---

1. Winning The Money Game: Lessons Learned from The Financial Fouls of Pro Athletes. Adonal Foyle, 2015, Harper Collins Publishers.

for two years while they established their financial bearings. Lynn adds that while she was not tied to the hockey lifestyle, it was still a big change, and she had to adjust quickly.

Grant Clitsome said that he felt a spouse could help her partner most by keeping communication open and by encouraging her husband to try different avenues in an effort to find a new passion. And he offered some "don't dos." He said a spouse shouldn't push her partner too hard in finding his next venture, and that she shouldn't feel too sorry for him, and as a result, try to do too much to help.

Chapter 10

What Advice Would You Give to Others Planning to Retire?

It's not surprising that players and wives who've been through it would have some great advice to offer to others who were nearing retirement from their sport. And they did!

- Don't think of the end of your playing career as a dead end; think of it as a crossroad.

Because it is truly a crossroad, one is forced to look in a different direction before proceeding; you can't simply charge

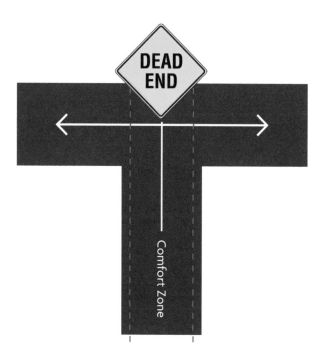

forward as you always have in the past. That means thinking outside the box, stepping out of your comfort zone. It means finding a new passion—something meaningful and fulfilling that will capture your imagination, and at which you can be successful, assuming you're prepared to work as hard at it as you did to become a successful professional athlete.

How do you do that? Well, according to the experts we consulted, there are several strategies available. First, they said, it's important to separate yourself from the game. That is, to acknowledge that you're much more than just a pro athlete. You're a successful person who, through determination, devotion to a long-term ideal, and a commitment to continual personal improvement, has reached the pinnacle of the sport you love. These skills and attributes can be transferred to virtually any other occupation you choose.

A second piece of advice in this regard was, "Don't fall in love with the game, and expect it to love you back." The game has no heart, and is incapable of returning the love you might have had for it. Many players feel that they've given their heart and soul to it (and they have), and that at the end of their careers the game should show them some love. It won't happen. Neither the NHLPA nor the NHL Alumni Association have established any "exit protocol" for retiring players, meaning you won't even receive a phone call from either of those groups asking how you're doing. So move on, plan the next phase of your life, and don't allow yourself to be held hostage.

Third, be aware of the fact that you'll quite likely have several careers throughout your life, not just the one you choose after hockey. According to workopolis.com, only 30% of people stay in any one job for more than four years, 73% of Canadians have had more than four jobs in their career, and 57% have had more than five. Careers-advice-online.com says, "Career change statistics (in the U.S.) suggest that the average person will be making a career change approximately 5-7 times during their working life." Remember that Babe Ruth, one of the most successful hitters of all time, was successful in only one of every three trips to the plate. So go ahead, explore your options, try internships, shadow people whose businesses are interesting to you, and don't be afraid to "strike out" every once in a while.

Jackie Rafter, Founder and CEO of Higher Landing, a firm that provides transition assistance for professionals, athletes and executives who are determined to reinvent their career, made a shrewd observation on the topic of exploring new careers. She noted that often, retired pro athletes are hired into sales positions by firms who wish to leverage the player's profile in order to build their business. But those situations rarely work out successfully. The reason is that players are generally most comfortable and thrive in a "team" environment, not usually in a sales position where they are often uncomfortable and feel alone.

Remember the comments above stating that one of the things players miss most in retirement is the camaraderie of the dressing room, and the feeling of team cohesiveness?

Chris Kontos and Tyler Sloan are good examples of players who were impacted by this feeling. Chris initially found work in a television station, which he really enjoyed because he was reporting on sports; working with the news team reminded him of his playing days, and made him comfortable. Tyler, on the other hand, took a directional drilling sales job in the oil and gas industry in Calgary. While it allowed him to build his network and get used to a normal 9-to-5 job, he was "pretty miserable for a whole year." There was little or no "team" aspect to the job, so he gave it up and searched for other opportunities.

Our experts also commented on the fact that the challenge they found in retirement was as much psychological as it was financial; that it was important emotionally to find a job you love and can commit to as soon as possible after retiring. It's important, they said, to prove to yourself that you have skills that can be transferred from your sporting career to a new career. That's another reason why they felt that the retiree should get on with it quickly after calling it a career.

The first thing every athlete leaving the game should prioritize is what skills they can add to their life. In fact, going back to school is the best thing a guy can do in his first year away from the game. For most guys, formal education ended at 16. In the NHL, there's very little time for reading. In fact, on game days, your phone can't even be in your hand from the time you get to the rink to the time you leave the locker room. So no iBooks, no reading financial news, or answering

emails. Some teams even extend this no-phone rule to practice days. The unspoken culture is "don't think about anything but hockey."

If going back to school isn't in the cards, you still need to put yourself in a situation so you can start acting like a regular person. Go get a job. Work part-time if you have to. Let's say a guy gets a job as a manager of a restaurant. A lot of useful life skills come out of that job that you were never exposed to as a pro hockey player. You're managing a team, working with people and learning about balancing cash, but the most important thing about a civilian job is how it centers you and humbles you so you don't need to be the guy that put the jersey on anymore. It allows you to escape the "character" you were on the ice. You're not him anymore.

—Sean Avery

• Stay busy; be proactive.
Virtually every player (and their spouse) emphasized this point. They encouraged others to fill the "hole" with purposeful activity: work out (it creates good endorphins), play pick-up hockey to recreate the dressing room and team atmosphere you miss so much, find a new outlet for your athletic abilities and your competitive spirit. And they urged others to "take the scary step": step outside your comfort zone, and explore, explore, explore.

"Depression is real...for retired players. It's the one thing that validates you, and now you don't have that. The game, this make-believe-world we have been in, consumes you and as a result of that, you don't necessarily have time to develop skills for the real world. For me, I'm going to stay busy."

—Grant Hill, seven-time NBA All-Star who played 19 years in the pros.

• You'll definitely feel alone when you retire; so build a support network in advance.

"Guys get depressed. It's like you're lost. It's like who are you? You have to have a strong will, strong support system and you have to have stuff going on that keeps you busy."

—Former NBA All-Star Baron Davis who retired in 2012 after a 13-year career.

Almost invariably in our conversations with players, they expressed feelings of abandonment and loneliness immediately after retirement. This was still true, though to a lesser degree, even by those who had a corps of non-hockey friends to help them in their transition. Several players felt they'd been abandoned by the NHLPA, who they thought could and should have reached out to them to offer support and if necessary, help. All acknowledged that their agents dropped them as soon as they were no longer generating revenue for them.

Steve Montador felt completely abandoned and alone.

Pavel Kubina reported that he's never received even a single phone call from anyone at the NHLPA or the Players Alumni Association since he retired nearly two years earlier. Daniel Carcillo, who expressed his frustration with the Players Association after the death of his friend Steve, commented in our conversation that as of two full months after he retired (in mid-September, 2015), no one from the Players Association had called to see how he was doing. And he wasn't doing well—he struggles with all the challenges of transition we've discussed so far.

Several other players were less forthright in their criticism, but acknowledged that there's lots of opportunity for improvement in the level of support currently being offered to retiring players by their Association.

So if he's on his own, what should a player do?

The consensus was that he should build his own network during his career, including friends, one or more mentors (who could provide internship or job shadowing opportunities), a support group, and perhaps seek assistance from a therapist after retirement.

Several players commented on how helpful their local chapter of the Alumni Association had been as a place where they could network, seek advice from others, and learn that others too were experiencing the same fears, doubts, and insecurities as they were.

While many spouses were eager to assist their husbands, and did all they could, players felt that it's simply not realistic to expect a spouse to possess all the experience and professional know-how required to effectively address the variety of issues and challenges a player faces during the transition.

On the topic of networking, the results of a survey conducted among NHL players found that the guys who are already doing it are creating a protective effect for themselves, reducing stress, and they are less worried about being traded or losing their jobs. "The trick is to get the guys out of their hockey bubble," said the study's co-author. "They have a chance to leverage opportunities while they still have the jersey on their back." But it diminishes the moment he retires.

On the topic of networking, the results of a survey conducted among NHL players found that the guys who are already doing it are creating a protective effect for themselves, reducing stress, and they are less worried about being traded or losing their jobs. "The trick is to get the guys out of their hockey bubble," said the study's co-author. "They have a chance to leverage opportunities while they still have the jersey on their back." But it diminishes the moment he retires.

• Stay in the game as long as you can contribute.
The advice here focused on taking your job as a player seriously, staying in shape: "Your body is your company; you are the CEO," and not taking your career for granted in any way. This addressed the issue that so often came up where

players regretted the fact that they might have quit too soon, or that had they taken it more seriously, they might have been able to lengthen their career. Cory Cross addressed this issue when he said that, in retrospect, he could perhaps have played a little harder, and a little longer. So the advice was to stay in the game as long as you can still contribute, get it out of your system, and then move on.

Mike Foligno took this approach, and as a result was able to walk away on his own terms with no regrets. While you're playing, he told his sons, focus on hockey completely, and don't be distracted by business ventures or other opportunities you may be offered. You can do some educational preparation while still playing, he said, and can put the pieces in place for future business interests, but don't be involved in business management or operations while you're still playing…it's too distracting.

• Be prudent in your approach to earning and spending money. There's an old saying that goes: "You can live like a king for a short time, or live like a prince for the rest of your life."

Those who've made successful transitions attribute a significant part of their success to the fact that they were prudent with their money, both during their career and in retirement.

Comments like these were common:

• Avoid "lifestyle overboards" and frivolous, expensive "toys."

- Be very wary about private equity deals such as restaurants, hotels, and vacation condos. Only about 3% of
  private equity deals turn out successfully for the investor.

- Avoid casual financial advice from the friend of a friend,
  or from your buddies. Get solid, professional help from a
  trusted lawyer, accountant, and financial advisor.

- Don't trust anyone 100%; trust, but monitor.

- Don't try to turn your millions into billions.

- Some players think that everyone wants to help them;
  what those people really want is the player's money to
  help themselves.

- Get your education first; you can still play pro hockey
  after college.

We noted earlier how there's a growing trend towards NHL
players coming from the college ranks. Not surprisingly, the
advice offered about getting an education first came mostly
from those who'd done so. As one of them said, "Get your
education first. You can still play pro hockey after earning
your degree. You can fall back on it after your pro career, and
it's not that heavy to carry around." It's much more difficult
for a player to pursue his formal education after his career
when he's in his 30s, quite likely married and with a family,
than it is before, when he's in his teens or early twenties, and
less likely to have a family to provide for.

• Don't forget that you have many "transferable skills."
As noted earlier, the research reports that athletes often see themselves as "one-trick ponies" who don't realize the transferable value of the wide range of skills they possess—skills that allowed them to perform at a world-class level. Our experience too, was that many of the athletes we interviewed short-changed themselves in this regard. But when athletes realize they already have the skills and characteristics to make them successful in non-athletic areas, they become empowered. Fortunately, some of those we interviewed emphasized this fact, and urged others to acknowledge it too. Who can argue that pro athletes possess organizational skills, adaptability and flexibility, dedication and perseverance, patience, self-motivation, the ability to perform under pressure, to meet deadlines, to set and attain long-term goals? And who can argue that these skills aren't important elements of success in virtually any career?

Planning for retirement from sport is somewhat akin to estate planning. Everyone knows that their lives will come to an end, but only about half of the population has taken the logical step of creating a will, and a far smaller percentage of the population has prepared a complete estate plan. Everyone should do it; most people don't. In the same way, pro athletes know their careers will come to an end. They should all plan for life after their sport; most don't because what they really want to do is continue playing. We hope that this advice from their peers won't fall on deaf ears.

"Your expert team stays on as you transition to retirement and a potential second career. At the time your agent leaves the picture, hangers on also leave. This is the time when you can feel alone if you don't have an expert team. Your wealth manager will encourage you to start thinking about what might interest you after your sports career. Use your fame while playing to meet people who can help you transition to a new career. Your expert team will help you plan for the big change of reduced income and not being in the spotlight. A transition plan will give you confidence as you enter into the next stage of life after sports."

—Francois Giguere, a 20-year NHL player and now a wealth manager.

Chapter 11

What Should Be Done to Help Players Transition into Retirement?

To put it bluntly, many players feel that the NHL Players Association and the Alumni Association could and should be doing a lot more to help them when they leave the game (there was considerable confusion as to the role each Association plays in this regard). While they give credit to both Associations for some of the recent initiatives that have been taken and for some of the programs already in place, the overwhelming feeling was that there's a whole lot more that should be done. One player noted that the Association's services are "few and far between," and several others echoed that comment.

A former player who is now a coach observed, "The Alumni Association seems to be more concerned about public relations and doing charity work to help the less fortunate in the community, than they are about their own members."

At the same time, many players acknowledged that they aren't taking advantage of the services that are already being offered, and also acknowledged that the primary responsibility for their post-career futures rests with them, not the NHL. The Alumni Association is, theoretically at least, in existence to help players after their careers are over. According to many players, however, it doesn't; not as much as it could, or should.

Player and spouse suggestions for additional services that

the Association could provide, that would be well received, included:

- Programs designed to help players improve their networking skills.
- Ongoing counseling sessions for both players and their wives which address the key challenges they'll face as they retire from the game (many of which are discussed in these pages).
- Education sessions which highlight the pressing need for players to consider options they may wish to pursue in retirement—visited before the inevitable end of their career.
- Internship and job shadowing programs that could allow players to explore future career opportunities during the offseason.
- Greater encouragement and facilitation of on-line university credits that players could enroll in during the year and/or in the offseason.
- A mentorship program which matches a player who's already retired and who volunteers to "buddy" with a player who's just retiring; this could include provision for the newly-retired player to receive a phone call from his mentor on a monthly basis during the first year of his retirement.

One player who requested anonymity spoke passionately on this topic. He said players are mostly too proud to pick up the phone and admit they need help or to ask for help, so the call must come the other way.

And he said, you can tell how a guy's doing by the tone of his voice in a conversation. "When I played," he said, "I spoke to 50 or 60 people a day; when I retired, there were very few phone calls. I felt alone and abandoned. Everybody moves on and you're left behind. Then guys get depressed, and start to do stupid stuff; a lot of them really struggle, but no one knows about it. In the three years I've been retired, no one from the Players Association has called me...even once. There's something wrong with that."

- Counseling services that offer players the opportunity to take job aptitude and interest tests, as well as tests which identify personality strengths. These could then be used in counseling sessions to assist a player to focus on specific career aspirations, and provide him motivation to seek further training, licensing, or certification. In today's world, these could be offered in a mix of on-line, small group and individual sessions.

With the help of former Vancouver Canucks scout Duncan Fletcher and Toronto-based headhunter and career management consultant John Hierlihy, the NHLPA began researching a personal development program in 2013 with a survey posted on its players-only website. 92 players took part in the survey and another 29 players were interviewed in-person or over the phone. According to the survey, 82.6% of respondents said they'd be interested in a personal development program while they were still active players. Roughly 75% of respondents said that they wanted to learn more about the finance and wealth management industry. Nearly 70% of players wanted more education about networking, while 65% of players said they wanted to pursue post-secondary education.

Chapter 12

Sources of Support Currently Available

The NHL Alumni Association: BreakAway Program

In November of 1999, the NHL Alumni Association was created as an independent, not-for-profit organization by amalgamating two Alumni groups that had previously been formed by the National Hockey League (NHL) and the NHL Players Association (NHLPA). The Alumni's ties to both the NHL and the NHLPA remain strong today.

The Alumni Association's stated mission is to:

1. Assist in youth hockey initiatives: involve former NHL players in support and participate in raising funds for charitable causes that enhance the quality of life for our youth.
2. Assist former NHL players in their transition to life after hockey.
3. Promote the great game of hockey and inspire today's youth through positive images as guardians of the game.

Wendy McCreary, Senior Director of the NHL Alumni and BreakAway (Career Transition) Program told us in December 2015, that these priorities will soon be re-ordered on the website, making current item #2 (Assist former NHL players in their transition to life after hockey) its #1 stated priority.

According to the Alumni Association, it maintains a database of the approximately 3,400 living retired players (of just over 5,300 who have ever played in the NHL), and the 1,600 who are currently registered and active with the Association. It calls itself "Hockey's Greatest Family."

The BreakAway Program

The best-known offering available to retiring NHLers is probably the BreakAway Program (formerly known as the Life After Hockey Program). It's funded by the National Hockey League Players' Association and the National Hockey League, and administered by the NHL Alumni Association.

Based on the information available on its website, the Break-Away Program offers a wide and impressive array of services to its members. Among the key components are:

Counselling
Counselling services are provided by a team of qualified professionals offering cognitive-behavior therapy for sleep problems, stress, anxiety, depression, addiction, marital problems, and post-injury trauma.

Entrepreneurial Training and Assistance
The BreakAway Program provides players with the tools and confidence they need to evaluate specific business opportunities. Its customized entrepreneurship course (available for credit or non-credit) can be taken on-line or in a classroom setting.

Education
With an education consultant on staff to assist, players can select from continuing education degree courses (through Ryerson's Chang School of Continuing Education or McGill

University) or non-degree certification courses (through Ryerson's Ted Rogers School of Management) where courses such as Basic Principles of Personal Finance, Basic Principles of Marketing, and Personal Branding and Social Media are available.

After an 11-year NHL career, mostly with the Buffalo Sabres, Ric Seiling commented positively on some of the Alumni's offerings. He said, "I've taken a lot of courses. The NHL Alumni started a program for life after hockey. I took public speaking, business management, broadcasting and put myself through a Dale Carnegie class. All those things combined to help me develop into what I'm doing today."

After an 11-year NHL career, mostly with the Buffalo Sabres, Ric Seiling commented positively on some of the Alumni's offerings. He said, "I've taken a lot of courses. The NHL Alumni started a program for life after hockey. I took public speaking, business management, broadcasting and put myself through a Dale Carnegie class. All those things combined to help me develop into what I'm doing today."[1]

Career Exploration and Transition Assistance

Finding a new career that ignites a passion similar to professional sport can be a daunting task. BreakAway offers customized one-on-one and group transition services for retired athletes looking to explore and prepare for new careers.

1. http://playershelpingplayers.com/News/ric-seiling-sabre-fought-early-retirement-1

As part of the service, utilizing a team of coaches and con-
sultants who specialize in working with professional athletes,
clients are offered personalized business and/or retirement
sessions that explore topics from developing your network
and updating your resume, to interviewing and negotiating a
job offer.

One-to-One Business and Life Coaching

Working with NHL Alumni who are offering these services,
they can assist the retiring athlete by:

- Identifying the roles and accomplishments that have
  given you the most satisfaction, and determining which
  of these many skills that made you and elite athlete are
  transferable to your new opportunities.
- Discovering your greatest personal strengths.
- Building on those strengths to ensure success in career or
  business ventures you might wish to explore.
- Conducting an inventory of your key interests and characteristics, allowing you to better market yourself.
- Determining how closely aligned your current situation
  is with your deepest values, interests, and competencies.
- Understanding the work roles and environments that
  you should avoid to reduce the danger of burnout and
  work dissatisfaction.

Mentorship Program

Past and present NHL players, like all professional athletes,
possess a wide variety of competencies, transferable skills,
and unparalleled experiences related to teamwork, leader-
ship, perseverance, and discipline. What they often lack is

first-hand work experience.

The Mentorship Program is a unique, online, social networking tool enabling current players and alumni to seek expertise regarding careers, support, and guidance in their local
cities worldwide. It's a community to make connections with
mentors, alumni, and friends of the NHL who have experience in various industries and careers. Registration in the
program can lead to internships, job shadowing, and full-
time jobs that are posted by connected mentors worldwide.

"Fraying at the Seams"

With this range of programs available to current and retired
players, why is it that, according to a Globe and Mail article
published in November of 2013, the NHL Alumni Association
is "fraying at the seams"?

While much of the dissatisfaction surrounds issues of gov-
ernance and transparency of the Association, the dissenters
also raised concerns that the alumni are slow to respond to
members seeking help form the NHL's emergency assistance
fund, which provides financial help to former players in need.

Mark Napier, Association Executive Director acknowledged
that there are communication problems associated with the
fact that the members of the family are scattered across
North America. One of these is that due to privacy reasons,
neither the NHLPA nor the NHL hands over contact information to the Alumni Association, which operates independent-
ly from the union and the league. As a result, it's up to the
retiring player to contact the Association. And, he adds,

many ex-players aren't diligent about providing that information, or about passing along subsequent address changes. As for funding, no dues are charged to members, requiring the Association to raise its operating expenses through sponsorships with companies such as the Bank of Nova Scotia and PokerStars.com. The result is that considerable energy must be expended each year just to keep the Association afloat, thus diverting attention from broadening the support services it might otherwise be able to offer its members.

Ian Turnbull, a former Toronto Maple Leaf and Los Angeles King defenceman (who now lives in LA) summed up the problem by saying, "If nobody tells you what's available (in alumni programs), there's something wrong. That's the essence of what this is about."

Others have said they feel that when players retire, there should be a system in place ensuring that they receive regular monthly telephone or personal contact from the Alumni Association during the first year of their retirement. That's often the time when players find the transition most difficult, and the time when such contact would be most helpful. But for now, the player is required to make the first call to ask for help or to tell someone of their personal struggles. Not surprisingly, relatively few of these proud individuals make the call.

A Tipping Point?

Following the death of Steve Montador in early 2015, his former teammate Daniel Carcillo declared in an online video that the NHLPA simply hasn't done enough to help its members move on with life after the game.

He commented that when he asked fellow players what the exit program was for NHL players, no one knew. "Right now," he said, "as far as the PA (Players Association) goes, we would receive a phone call to see how we're doing and that's pretty much our exit program." But speaking to Carcillo two months after he announced his retirement in September, 2015, he told us he hadn't received a single phone call from the PA: "It just pisses you off and makes you angry that no one calls."

Wendy McCreary confirmed that no formal NHLPA or Alumni Association "exit protocol" exists at this time.

"From the guys that I've talked to who have moved on, they've all said the same thing. All fell into a deep depression and went away quietly. It was almost the less noise you make when you go away, the better. I don't think it's right. It doesn't feel right for how much we give this league and this sport. Sacrificing our bodies, sacrificing our minds with the concussions and the hits we take."
—Daniel Carcillo

In the face of such comments, the outcry arising from the death of Montador and the passing of former players Wade Belak, Derek Boogard, and Rick Rypien during a four-month period in 2011, the NHL and the NHLPA announced the imminent creation of an individual player development program aimed at better preparing its athletes for they issues and challenges they face after hockey. NHLPA executive Mathieu Schneider said, "What we want to do is enable guys to be able to do whatever they might want. Similar to what you probably have as a guidance counselor, whether in high school or college. Guys come into the league particularly young and we want them to think about their life outside sport."

The NHLPA and the NHL will split the initial cost of the program's first three years, each contributing a little under $1.5 million toward whatever education, mentorships, or apprenticeships are sought by players. Clearly, not every player deals with mental health issues, concussions, or addiction, which is why the NHLPA will look to assist players in other areas too, such as helping them find outside interests and managing their income.

At least on paper though, several initiatives identified under this new plan are already available through the Alumni's BreakAway Program. This raises the question of whether the announcement is merely an attempt to throw money at a not-widely-understood program in the hope that the furor will soon die down.

It's interesting to note too, that several aspects of the programs and initiatives requested by players in Chapter 11 above look very much like components of the existing BreakAway Program as described on its website. This suggests either that the NHLPA/Alumni are not doing a very good job of informing their members of the programs available to them, or that the players are not very diligent in informing themselves of what's available to them through their union.

One would hope and expect that the NHL Alumni Association (Hockey's Greatest Family), with a stated goal of "assisting former NHL players in their transition to life after hockey," would be seen by NHL alumni as a source of strong support and assistance as they transition to their next career. But our conversations with many retired players indicated that this is simply not the case. In fact, in announcing the "new" program, Mathieu Schneider is quoted admitting, "There's no question it's been neglected for a long period of time. I know there are numerous reasons, but I can say particularly from the players' association (side), we were going through years of turmoil and turnover in executive directors, and it was probably an extremely low (priority) internally with all the political struggles that were going on." That's a truly astounding admission that probably goes a long way to explaining why the players are as disgruntled with the Alumni Association as they are.

Player discontent with the NHLPA and the Alumni Association has been simmering for several years. Perhaps the death of Montador, the public statements made by Carcillo, the widespread support he's received for his initiative among the players, and the PA's admission that not enough has been done, along with its commitment to this "new" program, will represent a tipping point in recognizing the need to provide more support and assistance for its retired players. Time will tell.

The Career Enhancement Program (CEP)

The Career Enhancement Program is operated by the Professional Players' Hockey Association (PHPA). It's the organization to which players in the 30-team American Hockey League (AHL) and the 28-team East Coast Hockey League (ECHL) belong. It is the PHPA's version of the NHL's BreakAway Program. The CEP provides career planning and personality testing, education at all levels from Grade 12 to graduate studies (in co-operation with Athabaska University), résumé and interview preparation and links to certification and licensing programs.

More recently it has added a Membership Assistance Hotline, which provides confidential, free, 24/7, consultation with professionally trained counselors in most cities across North America. Members can seek advice on topics such as depression, legal issues, relationship and parenting matters, addictions, stress and anxiety, financial management, and concussion management.

The CEP has also found support among its members for the firefighting course it sponsors in association with the Fire and

Sources of Support Currently Available

Emergency Services Training Institute (FESTI). It can be taken in part on-line, and in part in the summer at the Institute's facility located at Pearson Airport in Toronto. It also co-sponsors a Business Basics Online course with Niagara College.

The Association player-representative on each team is expected to be an ambassador for the program, and to encourage his teammates to take advantage of the programs and services it provides to its members. According to the Program Coordinator, about 1,500 members have participated in CEP offerings over the last 16 years. Like the NHL Alumni's BreakAway Program, the onus is on the player to make the first call; but unlike BreakAway, the CEP has an ambassador in the locker-room of every one of its nearly 60 member teams, educating and encouraging its members to utilize the services available to them.

Game Plan

This is a program for Olympic and Paralympic athletes and hopefuls, designed to help them transition to new challenges after sport. Hayley Wickenheiser, six-time Olympian, five-time medalist, and four-time gold medalist, serves as the program's spokesperson.
It includes five pillars to prepare for life beyond sport.

Career Management—a job board with flexible work opportunities for athletes so they can get work experience while training or competing.

Health—access to mental health support 24/7 and awareness training.

Networking—a mentoring program between experienced athletes and next generation hopefuls.

Education—specialized training opportunities and flexible class schedules at educational institutions.

Skill Development—conferences and webinars educating athletes on brand management, public speaking, and financial planning.

Hayley, like Daniel Carcillo, was moved by her friend Steve Montador's untimely passing, and like Carcillo, she wrote an article in April, 2015 in The Player's Tribune. It was entitled "Out of the Shadows." She too decried the lack of support available for retiring athletes whether they be pros or elite Olympic competitors. She said she'd received calls from both current and retired players in the weeks following Monty's death, and she said they called for two reasons: "They too are struggling, and they want to help other players in the game. For the guys who are retired, they are struggling with finding meaning after playing. For the guys currently playing, they are struggling finding meaning for what they are doing, and scared it could be them next." She says, "It takes courage, courage to reinvent and redefine yourself. Some athletes have the tools and the ability to do that without guidance, but many don't."

Her involvement in Game Plan is no doubt a result of her concerns about the lack of support currently available to transitioning pro and elite athletes.

"You are not what you do. We are so much more than what we do in life, but you wouldn't know that by reading your Twitter mentions after a bad game...It takes courage...to reinvent and redefine yourself. Some athletes have the tools and ability to do that without guidance, but many don't."
—Hayley Wickenheiser

The Canadian Sport Institute

The Canadian Sport Institute (CSI) is headquartered in Calgary and through its Life Services division, provides transition services to approximately 400 Olympic athletes who receive funding from Sport Canada and are registered with the Institute. The Life Services Manager, Cara Button, serves as a "gatekeeper" who meets with athletes, discusses their interests and needs, and then refers them to specialists in the appropriate field. She assists athletes with career planning and academic upgrading, and the Institute offers workshops on such topics as public speaking, self-branding, and networking. Qualifying athletes have transition counseling available to them for up to five years after retiring from their sport.

Cara made a couple of observations during our conversation that echo the experiences of others who provide similar services to elite athletes. She noted that in her 10 years she's found that while formal group programs look good on paper, they're a tough sell to athletes who, almost invariably, prefer one-on-one consultation. After all, throughout much of their careers, they've received individual attention from coaches, and seem to feel that they should be counseled one-on-one as well.

She also commented that the athletes' coaches aren't always fully supportive of these programs for fear that they may distract the athlete from their primary sport focus, though there are indications that this is beginning to change; some coaches are beginning to send their athletes to Life Services for discussions about life after sport.

She added, "Once an athlete is no longer receiving carding or retires from sport, we also try to connect with them to see where they are at, what services they may need etc..." This is an initiative that needs to spread to other service and support providers like the BreakAway Program and the Career Enhancement Program.

There were three key takeaways from this conversation. First, group programs aren't always as effective as might be anticipated; elite athletes are often reluctant to share their fears, concerns, or shortcomings in a group setting. Second, athletes are more likely to open up to an advisor or counselor in one-on-one situations—that's what they're used to. And third, athletes are often unwilling (or unable) to seek help from others; therefore, those who wish to assist must take the initiative and make the first call.

This seems to be the missing link in the programs we examined. In the two biggest programs we examined, the NHL's BreakAway Program and the PHPA's Career Enhancement Program, the onus is on the player to make the first call asking for help. Perhaps it's not surprising that neither program is seen as being as effective as it might be.

The Chapter 5 Foundation

"Why do NHL players struggle so much with moving on from the game? Why are so many former players I know battling depression? Why does the hockey community ignore them when they're gone? And why can't we create a more concrete program to help transition into real life?"

On the day Carcillo posted his video in April 2015, he felt a sense of relief because he'd put his message out to the world. He expected to be criticized for doing it, but just the opposite happened. He was overwhelmed with positive feedback through phone calls, text messages, and social media. The support reaffirmed in his mind that he had done the right thing.

His intention in posting the video was to start a conversation, thinking that some past and present NHL players may contact him, but he never expected other professional and elite athletes to reach out. When they did, it dawned on him that there's a real desire by athletes from all sports to be assisted in the next phase of their lives, and a feeling that it's just not happening now. That's what he says motivated him to create a non-profit organization to help guide athletes into the next phase of their lives. It's called Chapter 5—after the number that his friend Steve wore while playing in Chicago.

"I wouldn't have done that video if something was in place, obviously if Steve didn't pass away, there's so many factors that happened," Carcillo said. "It just felt like the right thing to do. I'm a big believer in signs and kind of following them, and everything pointed to that direction."

Chapter 5 is still in its infancy at the time of writing this book, with much work still to be done before it's up and running. But one thing Daniel was adamant about when we spoke was that unlike the NHL's BreakAway Program where the player must make the first call, when Chapter 5 is operational, "We'll get in touch with them."
chapter5foundation.com

Higher Landing

This firm offers transformation assistance to professionals, athletes, and executives who are serious about reinventing their career. It uses a proprietary three-stage, results-oriented process that includes:

- Six, one-on-one transition self-discovery sessions introducing a process that connects head with heart and identifies strengths, values, passions, and purpose.
- A branding session with a design process that defines "you" as a brand, and prepares you to go to market.
- A marketing session-- the delivery phase that polishes your brand, develops a go-to-market strategy, and directly markets you to strategic prospects.

higherlanding.com

Sources of Support Currently Available

Live, Learn, Lead Canada

Gisele Bourgeois' firm offers counseling and life coaching services to corporations and individuals. She worked with and assisted Steve Montador as he struggled to transition from hockey to his next career.

livelearnleadcanada.com

Players Helping Players

This Foundation was created in November 2014, by Chris MacKeigan, a Kingston, Ontario businessman and hockey fan. It's devoted to helping former professional hockey players who need a helping hand, whether it be emotional, medical or financial. It expanded to the U.S. in 2015 to offer its services to all former NHL players. It plans to offer a growing range of services to assist players increase their post-career earnings.

playershelpingplayers.com

Why Don't Pro Athletes Take Advantage of the Support Services Available?

One theme we heard consistently when speaking with representatives of the BreakAway Program, the Career Enhancement Program, and the Canadian Sport Institute was that pro and elite athletes are reluctant to seek help. As we probed deeper into why this might be the case, we revisited our interview recordings. Based on those player interviews (some of which are referred to earlier in the text), it became clear that there are five major reasons.

1. They think they can do it (whatever "it" is) themselves, they have a high level of self-confidence and a certain sense of invincibility that leads them to believe they don't need help of any kind.

2. They think their careers will last forever.

Both of these reasons represent delusional thinking, of course, but they're very real in the minds of these elite athletes. While there's no research data to support this theory, anecdotal evidence suggests that trying to discuss things like retirement or support services that might be available (to assist with issues such as drug or alcohol abuse or depression) with anyone under 25 is like butting your head against a stone wall. The experts say it's not until later in their 20s or even 30s, that they might be more realistic in facing the end of their careers.

3. They're too proud to make the call asking for help, and currently, all the programs we examined that are designed to help them require that they make the first call. The solution seems so simple, and yet it remains unaddressed by the service providers.
4. They simply choose not to think about the end of their career; they're too focused on being at the top of their game now.
5. They continue to feel entitled to the one-on-one, personalized coaching and counseling services they've been afforded for most of their athletic careers, but these aren't always available post-career.

Chapter 13

Key Differences Between Athletic Career Retirement and Civilian Retirement.

There are several differences documented between retirement from pro sports and a more normal retirement experience. The first major difference is that, as I noted in *The Pro's Process: An Expert's Approach to Wealth Management for Professional Athletes*, the average employee works 35-40 years, earning a lifetime income of $1.5-$3.0 million, with peak earning typically in the five years preceding retirement. Pro athletes on the other hand, will have a career that averages about five years in length, during which they'll earn an average of $15 million, 70%-90% of which will be earned before the age of 35...playing a sport they love, and to which they've devoted much of their lives. The sudden loss of a large income along with the simultaneous loss of their dream job is in stark contrast to the more gradual withdrawal associated with civilian retirement.

A second important difference is this. Most people hold traditional administrative, managerial, sales, teaching, or trade jobs, or are in the professions—so-called "civilian" jobs. Generally, these people retire after 30, 35, or 40 years on the job, and mostly look forward to doing so. These folks begin their retirement in what we call a "vacation" mind-set. That's the period immediately following retirement when "bucket list" activities predominate. The electrician, the manager, the teacher, the accountant, or the dentist has planned retirement for several years, and has a list of things they want to do when they no longer have to be in the office, or on the job every day. These activities often involve fulfilling life-long dreams such as cruising the Mediterranean, or travelling to exotic locales. It can also involve (at last!) serious work on the golf game. Or maybe it's buying that longed-for sports convertible. It's really doing what you've wanted to do for a long time, but just never had the time for...until now.

Unlike most civilian retirees who eagerly anticipate retirement, pro athletes (as well as elite athletes who maintain their amateur status) do *not* look forward to the end of their careers. In fact, our research demonstrates clearly that they wish their careers could go on indefinitely, and that they direct their efforts towards activities that will allow their careers to last as long as possible.

Our research makes it clear though, that pro athletes almost never experience this phase of retirement. Here's why:

Unlike most civilian retirees who eagerly anticipate retirement, pro athletes (as well as elite athletes who maintain their amateur status) do *not* look forward to the end of their careers. In fact, our research demonstrates clearly that they wish their careers could go on indefinitely, and that they direct their efforts towards activities that will allow their careers to last as long as possible. As discussed above, several of our interviewees commented that, looking back, they regret quitting the game as early as they did-- adding that they believe they could have remained competitive for a period of from one to five years longer. The thought of retirement is anathema to most pro athletes, and as a result, the thought of anticipating retirement in a positive way is just not part of their mindset.

Former Chicago Black Hawk Daniel Carcillo said in an interview about the time of his retirement in September, 2015: "It's a very abrupt reality check when you get out of the game. You identify with being a hockey player and an athlete for so many years that you kind of not lose yourself, but you forget who you are as a person and what your interests were in high school away from hockey, and who your friends were."

A third major difference is that civilian retirees don't usually experience the same disruption to their identity as athletes do. Because elite athletes spend so much of their time dedicated to their sport at an early age, they may not allocate time to develop interests in other areas. This can result in a disruption of normal development where the athlete identifies his or her life exclusively with the role of athlete. As a result, when athletes retire from their sport, they may feel a sense of intense loss and disillusionment that prevents them from giving credit to the lessons and skills they've acquired throughout their athletic careers. Of course, the same skills that made them successful in sports will contribute to finding success in their post-athletic careers.

Former Chicago Black Hawk Daniel Carcillo said in an interview about the time of his retirement in September, 2015: "It's a very abrupt reality check when you get out of the game. You identify with being a hockey player and an athlete for so many years that you kind of not lose yourself, but you forget who you are as a person and what your interests were in high school away from hockey, and who your friends were."

A fourth significant difference is that athletes typically start and finish their careers at a relatively young age. At approximately the same time that athletes are ending high-level competitive sport, their peers are often beginning careers in other occupations, getting married, and having children. These comparative situations may add to the already inherent stresses felt in athletic retirement, since the athlete can feel "left behind" on several fronts.

Chapter 14

Three Periods of Retirement for Professional Athletes

A review of the current pop literature on the topic of retirement could lead one to the conclusion that virtually every retiree's experience is unique, that everyone who moves into retirement experiences it alone, and that there are few identifiable patterns or themes that can be used as guides to what to expect when you're retiring.

There are three identifiable phases of retirement for the professional athlete, and there are signposts along the way to guide us, if we are alert to them. But by looking into the phenomenon more deeply, we find that it's *not* all about our own highly personal experiences after all. There are three identifiable phases of retirement for the professional athlete, and there are signposts along the way to guide us, if we are alert to them. We've all heard of the book entitled, "What to Expect When You're Expecting." This section's subtitle could easily be "What to Expect When You're Retiring."

As a result of looking at retirement from pro sport as fitting into a predictable pattern, an athlete might be better equipped to understand the turmoil that results, whether caused by career-ending injury or the result of the individual's decision.

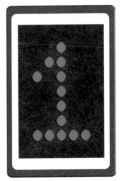

The 1st Period: Feeling Lost and Feeling Loss

For civilian retirees, when the "vacation" is over, reality reasserts itself, and suddenly they are faced with a "plunge into the abyss of insignificance." For many, confronting the reality of this "drop from the top" is one of life's top ten traumas. We typically spend the first 20 years or so of our lives being regimented, educated, preparing to be successful in our chosen field of work. Then we spend the next 30-40 years or more working, learning the rules and the ropes, rising through the ranks of our job or profession, taking on more responsibility, gaining credibility, and ultimately achieving considerable success and respect within our field.

For pro athletes, the transition is starker and more jolting. It goes from an intense career (lasting only about five years on average) with a highly-regimented lifestyle crammed full of training and conditioning, practice, personal coaching, travel, personal achievements, team success, and the camaraderie of the locker room—all augmented by rock-star popular adulation—to the day when it's simply over.

In the 1st Period, civilian retirees come face-to-face with the realization that for the remainder of their lives, there will likely be no more of the comfortable rhythms associated with their work life (the rhythm of the tax season for an accountant, the rhythm of the school year for a teacher or principal), and no more of the normal, comfortable routines. Such a realization is crushing for many, as their lives are simply turned upside down.

Pro athletes discover that one day, whether because of career-ending injury, personal decision, or team decision, it's simply over—and they feel lost.

Feeling lost, as many of us do in the 1st Period of Retirement, is the result of the fact that in this period, we suffer five significant, inevitable losses. We lose structure, identity, relationships, a sense of purpose, and a sense of power. And because these feelings are intensified in a relatively short pro career, the losses are more acute for athletes than may be the case in the retiring civilian population at large.

- We lose structure because our regular routines disappear entirely. Think of the routines associated with a pro athlete's life including training regimes, dietary discipline, prescribed practice schedules, tight travel schedules, and a lengthy seas on consisting of dozens and dozens of games. In retirement, these routines evaporate.

  To cope, we must replace an "other-directed" culture with a self-directed culture.

Ron Stern, a 12-year NHL veteran who played in Vancouver, Calgary, and San Jose before a back injury forced his retirement in 2000, described it this way: "You've had a coach for twenty-five years. The coach has told you when to eat, when to drink, how hard to work, when to go to sleep and what to do. It's a simple game to play: you work hard, you listen, you learn and you keep doing what they ask you to do."

Retirement means the end of that routine. The readjustment can be difficult for someone who punched a factory clock for forty years, and it can be particularly challenging for someone who's 35 to 40 years old and accustomed to the high-flying life of a professional hockey player. "You kind of lose your sense of direction," Stern says.

- We lose our identity. Because pro athletes are often associated with their sport, their team, and their individual or team accomplishments within their sport, this loss of identity can be particularly painful. Once they retire and are no longer seen in their team uniforms, they're generally no longer associated (in the public's mind) with their former pro-athlete persona. They're just guys on the street whom nobody recognizes any more.

  To cope, we must move from our previous social identity to a new, personal identity.

"I thought this life was going to last forever. As players, people come to us. We don't have to go to them. But guess what? Once it ends, unless you're Gordie Howe or Wayne Gretzky, nobody is looking for you any more."
—Corey Hirsch, 10-year veteran NHL goalie with New York Rangers and Vancouver Canucks

- We lose our formerly close relationships with our teammates, with team management, with the media, and with fans. Retired athletes report consistently that what they miss most about retirement is the camaraderie of the locker room, their relationship with their teammates, coaching staff, and training staff. Deprived of these tight relationships with people with whom they have spent extended periods of time during the season, and often over several seasons (their "band of brothers"), they often feel like fish out of water.

To cope, we must transition from previous results-oriented relationships to a future of heartfelt connections.

- We lose a sense of purpose. Pro athletes have often been raised from young ages to compete at elite levels, and to win. Much of their lives has been devoted to this end, and often involved their being away from home at early ages and for extended periods of time. But it was all sacrificed for the goal, for the purpose that made it all worthwhile: to win at the highest levels of their chosen sports. And then, sometimes suddenly, sometimes less so, it's over. The purpose that's driven them for much of their lives has come to an end. But their lives are, in many ways, just beginning. They're in their mid-20s to mid-30s, with 50 to 60 years likely ahead. Suddenly, they must recalibrate, set new goals, and find a new sense of purpose that can motivate them in their years ahead.

Easier said than done, but to transition successfully, we move from a success focus to create a personal vision for our future.

Three Periods of Retirement for Professional Athletes

"You have to re-find yourself and then re-purpose your life and kind of look inside you to what your second-best interest is other than hockey."
—Daniel Carcillo

"I didn't know how to be a regular person... It was very disheartening, but it helped me realize I had to find my next passion in life... I went through a time where I really had to think about who I am. Gymnastics was such a love and passion that to have that part of your heart taken away is really hard. I had to get into a rebuilding mode and be forward thinking. I had to set new goals without really knowing where they would take me."
—U.S Olympic gymnast Shannon Miller, whose career was over at age 19.

- We lose a sense of power. Normally, people achieve their greatest level of power or influence in the latter years of their working career. This power or influence often comes near the end of a long, successful career, and it can be devastating to an individual's sense of confidence and to their psyche when it's no longer a reality. So, with pro athletes who are often placed on pedestals by the press and the public, there comes a sense of power or influence. People attach importance to what they say and do, and how they behave. But as with the other losses outlined above, when they retire, pro athletes mostly fade from public view, often with a sense of diminished influence or power. In retirement, we must move from position power to personal power.

Three Periods of Retirement for Professional Athletes

Researchers tell us that 85% of people attach a strong sense of importance to the structure, identity, relationships, purpose, and power they receive from their jobs, and there's no evidence to suggest that pro athletes are much different in this regard. If anything, there's an argument that because of their larger-than-life image in the minds of the public, pro athletes might suffer these five inevitable losses more personally, and perhaps more hurtfully, than others do in retirement.

The losses associated with the 1st Period have been connected to bouts of depression, family stress (including family breakdown), alcoholism, drug abuse, and general misery, both in the general population and within the ranks of retired pro athletes. Many pro athletes are faced with the stress and pressure of a substantial financial loss in retirement. While their average salaries are substantially higher than those in the general population, after taxes, after agent's fees, after indulging in a perhaps "over the top" lifestyle during their careers, and after the well-documented investment losses suffered by a large number of pro athletes, the sudden realization that there will be no more big paydays can add to the other five losses experienced by retirees in the 1st Period. These, in turn, add to the feelings of isolation, stress, anxiety and depression documented widely in the research.

During an interview from his home in Calgary, Ron Stern observed that a period of "emotional transition" can be difficult. "Some guys get divorced and lose more than half of their money. They get into drinking

because they're unhappy, or drugs. They get into some sort of depression. It's the same challenge for wives. They're used to a certain lifestyle. The player is never around, so she can do what she wants. Retirement changes the whole environment. The kids wonder, 'Why is dad so grouchy?' It's because he doesn't know what he wants to do when he grows up." He said many retired players take three to five years to find something they enjoy doing.

In the 1st Period (before we achieve breakthrough results that are possible in the 2nd Period), we're going to go through a period where we feel a real sense of fear, uncertainty and anxiety. That's just the way it is! We can't skip any of the Periods and simply cruise on to the next. When people attempt to avoid or evade these feelings of fear, we see addiction rear its ugly head. The reason is that in order to move forward, we need confidence, and in the 1st Period it can often be in short supply, given all the losses we endure. A lot of people get their confidence through drug or alcohol abuse or some other harmful activity. There's a façade of confidence, but it's artificial. People know, deep down, that they have to move on with their lives and to grow. And they want to, but they're not entirely committed to it because they don't know what it looks like yet.

As a result, they're caught in a no-man's land where they feel fear, anxiety, and uncertainty, but don't have the capability to figure out what to do. So they retreat into a behavior— whether it's drug or alcohol abuse or other addiction—

Three Periods of Retirement for Professional Athletes

because it makes them feel good for a while, and it gives a superficial appearance of confidence and capability. But inside, they're a mess.

The losses associated with 1st Period are indeed huge losses for many. In the end, most of us seem to be able to adjust and cope. Without doubt though, it can be a very daunting challenge. But only after suffering the Five Losses do we begin to ponder what's really important and muster the courage (yes, the courage) necessary to move forward with our lives.

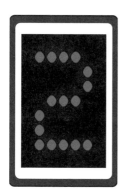

The 2nd Period: Experiments, Initiatives, and Rehab

"When you retire, you don't get rushed up to the front of the line. All that stuff starts to fade. That can add to some of the depression some of the guys feel. So the key is to find what you like and just stay busy."
—Brian Shaw, 14-year NBA veteran

In the 2nd Period, we begin recovery. According to psychiatrists and psychologists, two key requirements for human happiness are to be loved, and to have a sense of purpose. So the 2nd Period addresses the challenge of how retirees can get "back in the game," perhaps not their former game or profession, but into "the game of life" (which for many retirees will extend two or three decades into the future, and for retired pro athletes will likely extend five to seven decades ahead) with a renewed sense of purpose.

The 2nd Period requires experimenting with possible job opportunities, completing academic requirements, doing research that may lead to starting a new business, getting immersed in charitable activities, perhaps continuing with former work on a part-time basis. In the case of retired pro athletes, it might include exploring continued involvement in their former sport in a different capacity and at different levels (from coaching, to scouting, to management, to agency activity). Our research confirms that the 2nd Period often involves "false starts," where things seem initially promising, but then turn out to be "no go." Retirees who have success- fully navigated the 2nd Period report that false starts are to be expected and are entirely normal.* But each false start can be educational, if only in identifying areas that should likely not be explored further. They can also assist in helping one narrow their focus on specific areas of interest, until the right thing presents itself.

*(Hockey players hope that every shot they take will result in a goal. In fact, less than 10% of shots on goal in the NHL actually score. We looked at the 2014-15 NHL season and dis- covered that during that entire 82-game season, there were 73,595 shots taken on goal, but only 6,549 goals scored. That means only 8.9%...fewer than 1 in 10 shots on goal turned into goals. But that didn't stop players from taking their shots in the hope that the next one would be a goal. And so it is with retirement. Expect there to be several false starts when

you explore options for future work, but at the same time, remember the next shot might be the goal you were hoping for.)

"I think you have to try a number of different things to figure out what you like, what you don't like, what you can do and maybe what you can't do."
—Grant Hill 19-year NBA veteran

Choosing initiatives or experiments that reflect one's own experience, expertise, or areas of interest are also more likely to lead to successful outcomes, and to clarifying a new sense of purpose which can propel us forward into the future.

Because not all experiments in the 2nd Period are successful, we sometimes see people give up on the 2nd Period and relapse to the 1st Period with its attendant darkness. Others keep plugging, looking for ways to contribute. Those who do so, and finally break through to the 3rd Period are the happiest, most satisfied, and most fulfilled of all the individuals we have tracked.

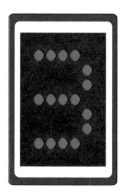

The 3rd Period: Breakthrough to a New Sense of Purpose

Successfully overcoming the challenges and confronting the losses and disappointments described in the previous periods of retirement can bring a wonderfully satisfying sense of accomplishment, fulfillment, and success in the 3rd Period.

Our research, and my own personal experience, has convinced me that in order to achieve the breakthrough that's possible, each of us must first wrestle with and satisfactorily answer this one fundamental question:

What is my LIFE PURPOSE?

Determining our life's purpose can be made easier by addressing these two lead-up questions:

- What is my unique ability?

  What are my personal strengths, special qualities, and talents?

  What are my favourite activities?

  What do I love to do most?

- What are my life's high points?

  What was highly gratifying during my career?

  What was I doing to create these high points?

  What were my creative abilities at the peak of my career?

When we isolate the common threads running through an analysis of our unique ability and our "high points," we're very close to identifying our LIFE PURPOSE.

In most cases, we know that one's life purpose tends to be found at the point where passion, unique skills, and the desire to make a difference in the world intersect. I call this intersection our "Sweet Spot," and once we identify it, future decisions, initiatives, and commitments become very clear.

Three Periods of Retirement for Professional Athletes

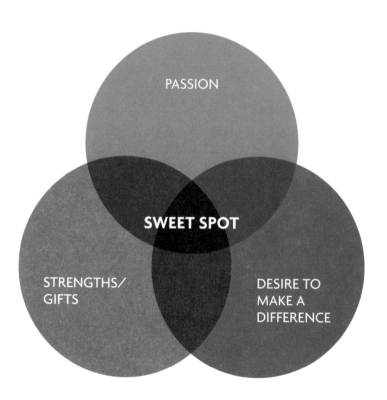

To Review:

1. Remember that you're not alone as you transition to retirement. At the time of this writing, approximately 10,000 North Americans are retiring every day!

2. You have more options to consider, and longer to do it than ever before. There are many resources to which we can refer you to provide guidance and counseling as you consider those options

3. You have a huge opportunity to combine your passions and your proven strengths to find a new purpose for your life, and to make the world a better place. To BE the change you'd like to see in the world.

And when you do, you'll discover that you've created:

- A new STRUCTURE for your life; one which you create for yourself, not one created and imposed on you.
- A new personal IDENTITY, connected to your passion.
- New RELATIONSHIPS, based on heartfelt connections.
- A renewed PURPOSE, a personal vision for the future.
- A sense of enhanced personal POWER to make good things happen for you, your family, and others.

The English Institute of Sport has identified the problems faced by retiring pro athletes as part of its Performance in Sport Program and wisely makes help available that athletes need. Its program is based on the Elizabeth Kubler-Ross Model for dealing with the five stages of grief and is applicable because in a very real way, retirement represents the death of many things for an athlete.

Denial, anger, bargaining, depression, and acceptance are concepts an athlete must transition through before they can move on. The last stage, acceptance, is often the hardest one because athletes are trained to overcome, not simply succumb to their fate. All athletes want to enjoy success in their professional life, but to enjoy it and live thereafter sometimes requires as much courage and application as getting it in the first place.

See the Appendix for more on the Kubler-Ross Model.

Chapter 15

Ingredients of a Successful Career Transition

What clearly emerges from the anecdotal and the empirical evidence is that those who cope best with the problems of sporting retirement are those who at least give some thought and planning to it before they bow out.

The literature doesn't clearly define or accurately measure factors related to successful athletic career transition, though it does provide some direction. The nearly 250 years of pro experience our interviewees shared with us have been much more helpful. They've enabled us to clearly identify the following factors that typically contribute to a successful transition.

1. Anticipation and preparation.

    For the most part, the athletes we interviewed chose to believe (to wish?) that their careers would go on forever, that they'd continue to earn big salaries, and that they'd experience few financial or occupational worries after the game. At the same time, they feared that if they actively prepared for a post-career life, it would detract from the focus they wished to maintain on being the best they could be at their sport, and that it could turn out to be a self-fulfilling prophesy: the equivalent of admitting defeat and failure. As a result, with few exceptions, there was little anticipation of, or preparation for, life after retirement on the part of those we interviewed. Notwithstanding this lack of anticipation and active preparation by the majority of our interviewees, several of them felt that they were nonetheless able to make an ultimately successful transition.

On the other hand, those who did some preparation found the transition out of sport somewhat less disruptive and traumatic. They more quickly created a new passion and challenge for themselves into which they could channel their energies. They also tended to have other interests and participated in a wider variety of outside-sport activities both during their playing days and after retirement. This finding supports the importance of encouraging athletes to maintain balance in their life by pursuing other interests and interests while engaged in competitive sports.

What clearly emerges from the anecdotal and the empirical evidence is that those who cope best with the problems of sporting retirement are those who at least give some thought and planning to it before they bow out.

2. Moving on quickly.
   They were the ones who were able to adjust to their new reality most quickly, to refocus their personal or professional commitments, and to get on with the next chapter of their lives. The more quickly they could do so, the quicker they regained their equilibrium, their sense of purpose, and their happiness. Whether because they'd decided on a new business or career path before leaving the game, or because they at least felt confident in their ability to do so shortly after retirement, those like Eddie Olczyk, who were able to spend the least time in the 1st Period, tended to have the fewest psychological challenges.

When the New York Rangers won the Stanley Cup in 1994, star Eddie Olczyk took it to the racetrack. A photo of him with that year's Kentucky Derby winner, Go For Gin, with his snout inside the Cup is a prized possession for Olczyk, a former Toronto Maple Leaf centre. His love for racing is as strong as his love for hockey.

Olczyk attended the races as a teenager growing up in Chicago, but it wasn't until he signed with the Leafs for the 1987-88 season that he jumped head first into ownership. In partnership with another Leaf player, Gary Leeman, Olczyk bought horses at auction and claimed a few from races. One of their fillies won five races.

In 1994, when the photo of Go For Gin was taken, hockey was headed for another work stoppage. During a visit to New Jersey's Meadowlands racetrack, Olczyk signed on to be the in-house simulcast handicapper and radio show host. He'd work on picking winners for the track for nine months.

Now retired and a member of the U.S. Hockey Hall of Fame, Olczyk juggles hockey as a popular NBC hockey broadcaster, with horses.

3. A healthy self-confidence.
    Problems in retirement are often connected to a loss of identity and reduced self-esteem, which translates to a loss of or diminished level of self-confidence (see Three Stages of Retirement—1st Period). With reduced

self-confidence, we become particularly fragile and vulnerable. Many athletes become dependent on sport for their identity and measure their self-worth by their ability as athletes; when they're no longer able to compete at an elite level, their self-image and self-confidence can be bruised--if not shattered. Where this is so, they often experience difficult transitions, and become confused about their identities and their future capabilities.

Those athletes who are aware: who can see how the many lessons and skills they acquired and developed during their athletic career can be transferred to their next career, are generally better able to retain a higher level of self-confidence. And the greater the degree to which they're able to protect their self-confidence and explore alternative future role possibilities, the greater likelihood of a successful transition out of the sport.

4. Strong self-management skills.
    The vast majority of our interviews included reference to the fact that, as a pro athlete, your routine is highly regimented. You're told when to rise in the morning, when to have breakfast, what to eat, when to practice, what time to meet the bus for a game or a flight, what time it's "lights out," and so on. As a result, players can become dependent on others for matters of personal management too, and as a result often lack the skills they'll need to make alternate career decisions.

When retirement happens, often quite suddenly, players might feel that the rug has been pulled out from under them, that they're entirely on their own. Many players commented on how they felt when the structures and routines they were so familiar with (and even dependent on) were no longer there, and they had to create a new set of structures and routines in order to cope with the reality of retirement.

So while a comforting routine, such as the one outlined above, may be attractive during a player's career because it allows them to focus on their game, there will come a time when they have to step up, take control of their own time management, and create important new routines. As we described it in the Three Periods of Retirement—the 1st Period, you must replace an "other-directed" culture with a self-directed culture.

5. A robust social support system.
Strong emotional support from family and friends can most definitely ease the confusion and disruption that comes with the transition from a pro-sport career. Those athletes who'd previously established a core of friends who weren't part of the game, and whose association continued after retirement, enjoyed an easier transition than did those whose friendships were concentrated within the game, especially if those friends continued in the game. Further, our research discovered that those retiring players who didn't have an existing established support system often found it difficult to develop such networks after retirement, leading to heightened feelings of isolation.

6. A strong, independent, "low-maintenance" spouse.
    Several of the athletes who were most successful in their
    transition expressed deep gratitude for the fact that their
    spouses were strong, independent, capable partners who
    were "low maintenance," at least during the most diffi-
    cult periods of their transition.

    Over and over again, we heard stories from both play-
    ers and spouses who recounted the importance of this
    support. Spouses told us, for example, how they simply
    stepped in when their husband was most vulnerable
    and lost (through lack of a daily routine to which they
    were accustomed), and created a new routine for them
    to follow until they got their bearings. In some cases, it
    was as simple as making them responsible for picking up
    the kids at school at a certain time every day, or taking
    responsibility for other chores that were required for the
    smooth running of the family's schedule.

    They also told stories of how they reminded their new-
    ly-retired husbands of the multiple skills they possessed,
    which could be transferred to new ventures including
    perseverance, commitment to a long-term goal, ded-
    ication to teammates, and their demonstrated ability
    to consistently perform at a world-class level in their
    chosen field. Human beings don't always transfer the
    confidence they may feel in one aspect of their lives to
    another, and sometimes need to be reminded and en-
    couraged to realize the range of strengths they possess.
    Many supportive hockey wives in our sample played a

major role in helping their husbands face their futures with confidence, and their contributions were recognized and deeply appreciated by their mates.

Those lucky (or wise) enough to have married strong, independent, "low maintenance" partners (who were willing and able to provide the support necessary), found that, almost invariably, the dark times weren't quite so dark and the troughs of depression weren't quite so deep.

Some spouses, on the other hand, were simply "along for the ride" in good times. They tended to have no children, or if they had children, they had nannies or other child-rearing help. These spouses were best at taking care of themselves: frequenting spas, doing lunch and shopping, assuming that the good times would roll forever, that the money would continue to pour in, and bigger and bigger houses and cottages and chalets were their right.

When retirement came, their lifestyle was seriously impacted. The money stopped rolling in. The retired athlete was around the house much more, and when he experienced some of the challenges we've described, particularly in the 1st Period of Retirement, they were simply unwilling or unable to provide the support, understanding, and patience required to help their spouses through the dark times that most retiring athletes experience.

Conclusion

"A lot of guys wish they could get back to where they were, but that's the first thing that has to stop. And once you realize that all the things that allowed you to play your sport at the highest level—all the discipline and commitment and perseverance and talent-- will serve you well after you retire, you're ready to start training for the new season. It's the one called the rest of your life."
—Sean Avery, an 11-year NHL player

My purpose in writing this book was to help players understand that their careers will be comparatively short, that the rest of their life will be much longer than their pro career, and that they'll be doing themselves and their families a huge favour by preparing, both financially and psychologically, for their inevitable retirement from the game.

I hoped and believed that, by interviewing a number of pros and spouses who've been through the transition, and by asking them to share their experiences (both joyful and painful), some good, solid, practical, real-life advice would emerge that could be passed on to others facing the same inevitable transition. I hope you believe this goal has been achieved, and that you'll benefit from the experiences and the advice documented here. Further, I hope my friend Monty will feel that this project achieves at least a part of what he had in mind when we first discussed it more than one year ago.

Acknowledgements

I am truly blessed to be in the advisory business working with outstanding people. I don't see this as a job at all; it's my life and I love it!

To all of our interviewees, players and spouses: Thank you! Without you sharing your stories with us, this project doesn't get off the ground. I thank you from the bottom of my heart and appreciate it immensely. Your contributions will truly make an impact on those who follow you in the world of professional sports.

To all of my clients, thank you for believing in me and The Pro's Process™.

To the Montador family, Donna, Chris, Lindsay and Paul, stay strong and continue to Dream Big. I thank you for welcoming me into your lives and family.

To my Partners and staff at ONE Capital Management, Thanks for the ongoing support!

Richard Pyper and Chris Lack for their commitment and expertise on the insurance front. I could not protect my group as effectively without you.

Jeffrey Steinberg. Thanks for the support and guidance through this complex business world. I will not make a business decision without your input and advice. I am proud to call you a mentor, business partner and friend.

To Shannon Brown and Ayron Sequeira. Thanks for believing in the vision and working with me to shape the ONE Sports & Entertainment vision and path!

Aknowledgements

Mom, I love you very much and thank you for your nurturing and on-going support.

Riles, I am very lucky to have found my calling and am grateful that you helped me to do so. Your ability to take the vision and concepts that I have, and to translate them into words is truly amazing! I am proud to call you my Dad, Partner and Friend.

Sarah, you are the mother of my living legacy and a truly wonderful mom. Thank you for being the constant in my life, the calming factor, and the best partner in the world. The travel and the time away are difficult, but you continue to believe in me, and for that I will be eternally grateful. I would not want to be on this adventure with anybody else!

Riley, my little princess, you make me proud every day! You are so bright and always entertaining. You make my eyes sparkle every time you perform on the basketball court or on the stage! Continue to amaze and work to be the best person that you can be! I am so proud of you!

Charlie, my little buddy, you are an amazing sponge, quickly picking up on all sorts of skills. I love watching and playing with you any sport that you do....and the best is that you love them all! Keep up the great work, and continue to work to be the best person that you can be! I am so proud of you!

It has been a difficult journey since we lost Monty but I promised him that we would complete this project so that we can help others and keep his legacy alive. He always wanted to help people and if this project can raise awareness and spread the word of these challenges that professional athletes face, I'll have done my job.

Morrison Montador, your Dad was an amazing individual, he was thoughtful, caring and forever giving! He was a dear friend and we had some very deep and meaningful discussions. Some day I'll share some of the great Monty stories with you. Your Dad is looking over you every second of every day, and he is smiling with great pride and joy! Just remember this, DREAM BIG Mo Mo!

The proceeds of this book will go to charities that were near and dear to Monty's heart in his name.

To everyone reading this, remember to DREAM BIG!

Moynesy

Thanks also to the following people who spoke with us about their programs, each of which assist retiring pro and elite athletes transition to the next phase of their life:

- Gisele Bourgeois, Founder of Live, Learn, Lead Canada
- Daniel Carcillo, former NHL player and Founder of The Chapter 5 Foundation
- Cara Button, Manager, Life Services, Canadian Sport institute
- Larry Downes, Co-Ordinator, Carer Enhancement Program, Professional Hockey Players' Association
- Wendy McCreary, Senior Manager, NHL Alumni Break-Away Program
- Jackie Rafter, Founder, President, CEO, Higher Landing

Appendix

Player Interviewees (Partial List)

Daniel Carcillo
Played for five NHL teams over 10 years; won two Stanley Cups; retired in 2015; a close friend and teammate of Steve Montador in Chicago; established the Chapter 5 Foundation to assist players as they transition from the game.

Grant Carter
Played for three teams in the CFL during an eight-year career; Grey Cup winner in 1995; Eastern All-Star in 1998; retired in 2001.

Marc Chorney
Played for the Pittsburgh Penguins and Los Angeles Kings during his five-year career; named to the NCAA All-Star team in 1981; retired in 1985. We also interviewed his wife Lynn.

Grant Clitsome
Played for two NHL teams over a seven-year NHL career; named to the ECAC Hockey All Academic Team in 2008; retired 2015.

Russ Courtnall
Played for seven NHL teams during his 16-year career; played on the Canadian Olympic team in 1984; retired in 1999.

Cory Cross
Played for six NHL teams over 15 years; selected to play for Team Canada; retired in 2009. We also interviewed his wife Shannon.

Dave Farrish
Played on three NHL teams during his 14-year playing career; won a Stanley Cup in Anaheim in 2007; Head Coach in over 1,000 games in the AHL, IHL, and ECHL; currently assistant coach with the Colorado Avalanche; retired as a player in 1990.

Mike Foligno
Played for four NHL teams during a 15-year career; played more than 1,000 games in the NHL; created the Foligno Leap; retired in 1994.

Chris Kontos
Played for four NHL teams during a 17-year career; won a Silver Medal at the 1994 Olympics with Team Canada; retired in 1998.

Pavel Kubina
Played for four NHL teams during his 20-year pro career; played on the Czech national team winning a Bronze medal at the Torino Olympics; won threeGold medals at the World Hockey Championships; won a Stanley Cup with the Tampa Bay Lightening in 2003-04; retired in 2013.

Steve Montador
Played for six NHL teams during his 14-year pro career; retired in 2013 as a result of suffering several concussions; passed away in February 2015.

Sean O'Donnell
Played on eight NHL teams during a 21-year pro career; won a Stanley Cup with Anaheim; played more than 1,000 NHL games; retired in 2013.

Wade Redden
Played on four NHL teams over a 14-year career in over 1,000 games; represented Canada at the Winter Olympics in 2006; represented Canada three times at the World Hockey Championships; retired in 2013. We also interviewed his wife Danica.

Tyler Sloan
Played for two NHL teams in a 12-year career; won a Calder Cup with the Hershey Bears; retired in 2013.

Shaun Van Allen
Played with five NHL teams during his 17-year pro career; won Calder Cup (AHL) and was AHL's leading scorer in 1991-92; retired in 2004.

Todd White
Played for six NHL teams over a 14-year career; ECAC Player of the Year in 1996-97; retired in 2010.

Five Stages of Grief/ The Kubler-Ross Model

The Kubler-Ross Model (developed by Swiss psychiatrist Elisabeth Kubler-Ross in the 1960s and refined over the years since), presents a series of emotional stages experienced, initially by survivors of the death of a loved-one. The model was subsequently found also to be useful in situations of personal trauma, loss, or change, including loss of a job or income, the end of a relationship or divorce, drug addiction, the onset of a chronic disease, even some minor losses. Some athletes refer to their retirement from their sport as being akin to "dying," hence the model (also known as "the grief cycle") has been found useful in assisting athletes address the five stages of grief associated with their retirement. The five stages of grief as described in the model are denial, anger, bargaining, depression, and acceptance.

As a model, it can be useful as a possible guide to what to expect during the transition from the life of a pro athlete to the life of a normal person. People don't always experience all of the five stages. Some stages may be revisited, and some might not be experienced at all. Transition from one stage to the next can be more of an ebb and flow than a steady progression. The five stages are not linear; neither are they experienced equally by all. People's grief, and other reactions to emotional trauma, are as individual as a fingerprint. And yet the model has withstood the test of time, and seems to offer at least a framework of the feelings pro athletes (and others) might feel following the end of their career.

The Stages

The stages, popularly known by the acronym **DABDA,** include:

1. Denial—Denial is a conscious or unconscious refusal to accept the facts, or the new reality (my career is over). It's a defense mechanism and perfectly natural. In this stage, individuals believe the decision or determination is somehow mistaken and cling to a false, though preferable, reality.

2. Anger—When the individual recognizes that denial can't continue, anger is often displayed. People dealing with emotional upset can be angry with themselves and/ or with others, especially those close to them: friends, spouses, even children. Typical responses of a person in this phase might be: "Why me? It's not fair!"; "How can this happen to me?"; "Who's to blame?"

3. Bargaining—The third stage involves the hope that the individual can somehow avoid the cause of the grief or pain. Usually the negotiation for an extended life is made in exchange for a reformed lifestyle. People facing less serious trauma often bargain or seek compromise. A pro athlete facing the end of a career might say: "Just give me one chance," or, "I'll be in the best shape ever."

4. Depression—During this stage, it's natural to feel sadness and regret, fear, and uncertainty. It shows that the person has at least begun to accept reality. In this state, the individual may become silent, refuse visitors, and spend considerable time being sullen and mournful. We

compare this stage to Period 1 of our model.

5. Acceptance—Arrival at this stage is an indication that there's now some sense of emotional detachment and objectivity, allowing the individual to accept--if not em-brace--the inevitable. Phrases such as, "I guess it'll be OK," or, "I can't fight it, so I might as well make the best of it," or even, "Let's get on with it," suggest that this stage has been reached. We compare this stage to the 2nd and 3rd Periods of our model.

So while Kubler-Ross' focus was on death and bereavement, the grief cycle model is a useful perspective for under-standing our own and other people's emotional reaction to personal trauma and change, irrespective of cause.

AFTER THE GAME: PLAYER QUESTIONNAIRE

Thank you for agreeing to participate in our AFTER THE GAME Research Study.

Introduction

Please think about how you'll respond to the following questions in advance of the interview.

Please make notes as memory joggers in preparation for the interview. Any personal anecdotes or experiences that relate to the questions below will add "colour" to the narrative, so please feel free to include them.

DURING YOUR CAREER

1. How long did you play at the pro level?
2. How long have you been retired?
3. How old were you when you retired?
4. If applicable, what were the advantages of playing college hockey, as opposed to going the more traditional junior hockey route?
5. As you think back over your playing career, what were some of the "highlights" that stand out for you from that time?
6. What do you miss most?
7. To what extent (if at all) did you consider a career after retirement from the game, while you were still playing? Did you do any *pre-planning*? Or were you mostly focused on your pro career?
8. What advice (if any) did you receive from colleagues∕

coaches/mentors about preparing for retirement from the game while you were still playing?

AFTER THE GAME

9. Please describe the events leading to your retirement from the game.
10. What aspects of the transition to retirement from your sport did/do you find *most challenging or difficult*? Why do you think this is so?
11. Much of the research suggests that after retirement, one might feel that there's a "hole" in your life, or experience episodes of sadness, feel "flat," experience some depression, and/or a greater than normal alcohol consumption. To what extent did you experience these feelings?
12. In what ways did your retirement have an impact *on your marriage*?
13. In what ways did your spouse assist in your transition?
14. What aspects of the transition to retirement have you found *easiest* to handle? Why do you think this is so?
15. What *advice* would you give to players who are still in the game, about preparing for their retirement from it?
16. In your opinion, what could/should be done to assist players making a successful transition from the pro game to the "rest of their lives"?
17. Please tell me the story of your current career and how it developed.

Thank you for participating in our study.

AFTER THE GAME: SPOUSE QUESTIONNAIRE

Thank you for agreeing to participate in our AFTER THE GAME Research Study.

Introduction

Please think about how you'll respond to the following questions in advance of the interview.

Please make notes as memory joggers in preparation for the interview. Any personal anecdotes or experiences that relate to the questions below will add "colour" to the narrative, so please feel free to include them.

Should you prefer to write your responses and submit them to the interviewer, rather than discussing them during the interview, that's perfectly fine too. We're happy to receive your responses and comments in the format that works best for you.

1. In what ways did your spouse's retirement impact *your marriage?*
2. What aspects of his transition to retirement do *you* think was the biggest challenge for *him?* Why do you think this is so?
3. Much of the research suggests that after retirement, there might be episodes of sadness, feeling "flat," some depression, and a greater than normal alcohol consumption. Did your spouse experience any of these?
4. What aspects of his retirement was the biggest challenge for *you?*

5. In what ways do you think *you* were best able to help him make the transition?
6. Were you given advice by other players' spouses about retirement while your spouse was still playing? What kind of advice did they give?
7. If asked, what advice would *you* give to the spouse of a player who was preparing to retire?
8. Are there other hockey spouses you know who might be open to discussing their retirement transition experience with me?

What other comments, observations or advice would you like to offer about *your spouse's retirement experience?*

Thank you for participating in our study.

Selected Bibliography of Digital Sources:

Avery, Sean "Transition Season." *playerstribune.com.*
The Players' Tribune. 18 June 2015. Web.

Fornabaio, Michael "Post-Hockey Career Not Necessarily Easy Adjustment for Ex-Sound Tigers." *ctpost.com.*
Hearst Corp. 21 February 2010. Web.

Carcillo, Daniel "Gone." *playerstribune.com.*
The Players' Tribune. 23 April 2015. Web.

Domenichelli, Hnat "The Hockey Sickness." *linkedin.com.* DSI
Sports Agency. 2 June 2015. Web.

Gretz, Adam "Report: Blue Jackets' Jack Johnson
Caught Up In Will Allen's Ponzi Scheme." *cbssports.com.*
CBS Corporation. 7 April 2015. Web.

Lazarus, David "How the Rich Sometimes End Up Poor"
LATimes.com. Tribune Publishing. Web.

Martel, Judy "Pro Athletes: How to Navigate Short Careers,
Long Retirements." *Forbes.com.* RBC Wealth Voice. 17 July
2015. Web.

McKnight, et al, "Life After Sport: Athletic career Transition and Transferable Skills" *zoneofexcellence.ca.*
Journal of Excellence. Issue 13. 2009. Web.

Meserve, Stephen "AHL On The Beat: Shore
Takes The Road Less Traveled." *theahl.com.*
The American Hockey League, 3 December 2015. Web.

Moore, Steve; Moore, Andy. "Why Athletes Need A Personal Development Plan." *therugbybusinessnetwork.com*, Rugby Business Network, 14 February 2015. Web.

National Bureau of Economic Research. "Bankruptcy Rates Among NFL Players With Short-Lived Income Spikes Working Paper #21085" *actpathway.com*. Athlete Career Transition, April 2015. Web.

Pack, Joe "Exiting the Game: How the NHL's New Retirement Program Aims to Help Players in Their Post-Hockey Life." *vice.com*.Vice Sports, LLC. 8 September 2015. Web.

Powers, Scott "Carcillo Wants To Make A Difference For Players." *espn.go*.com. ESPN 15 May 2015. Web

Roberts, Daniel "16% of Retired NFL Players Go Bankrupt, A Report Says." *fortune.com*. Time Inc. 15 April 2015. Web.

Rush, Curtis "Corey Hirsch Rebounds In Life Thanks To A Tweet." *thestar.com*. John D. Cruickshank. 13 February 2015. Web.

Shoalts, David "NHL Alumni Association Is Fraying at the Seams." *theglobeandmail.com*. 29 November 2013. Web.

Schober, Jeff. "Ric Seiling: Sabre Fought Early Retirement." *playershelpingplayers.com*, Players Helping Players Foundation, 9 September 2015. Web.

Schwartz, Nick "The Average Career Earnings of Athletes Across America's Major Sports Will Shock You." *usatoday.com*. Gannett Company. 24 October 2013. Web.

Steele, Al "Critical Mistakes And Dangerous Trends Facing Current and Former NFL Players." *Viktre.com*. Viktre. Article originally found at: *www.trilogyathletes.com/critical-mistakes-and-dangerous-trends-facing-current-and-former-nfl-players/* Web.

Turner, Broderick "Former Players Say Kobe Bryant Must Work On Transition Game." *latimes.com.* Tribune Publishing, 6 December 2015. Web.

Vinton, Nathaniel "Wife Of Ex-NHLer Michael Peca Tells Jurors Of Horror Of Losing Millions In Savings During Trial Of Alleged Hockey Con Men." *nydailynews.com.* Mortimer Zuckerman. 9 May 2015. Web.

Whitney, Ryan, Tales From Abroad: Russia. *playerstribune.com*. The Players' Tribune. 11 January, 2016. Web.

Whyno, Stephen, "'You have to kind of re-find yourself': Life after hockey can be a 'very abrupt reality check' for NHL players." *nationalpost.com.* The Canadian Press. 2 September 2015. Web.

Wickenheiser, Hayley "Out of the Shadows."*playerstribune.com*. The Players' Tribune. 23 April 2015. Web.

"Finding A Life After the NHL." *nationalpost.com.* Postmedia Network, 18 October 2011. Web.

"Going For Broke: When Athletes Lose It All." *cbsnews.com*. CBS Corporation. 13 September 2015. Web.

"How Star Athletes Deal With Retirement: Financial Lessons" *Forbes.com*, Forbes Inc., 2012. Web.

"NFL Players Turned Entrepreneurs: Translating Skills Into Success." *Talleynco.com* Talley & Company. Web.

"The End Game: How Sports Stars Battle Through Retirement." *cnn.com*, Turner Broadcasting System, 7 January 2013. Web.

"What Broke Athletes Can Teach Retirees" *Forbes.com*, Forbes Inc., 2012. Web.

"When The Game Is Over: Transition for the Pro Athlete." *growcounseling.com*, Grow Counseling, 2013. Web.

Selected Bibliography of Print Sources:

Business Day; May 9, 2012; David Willis, "Help For Pro Athletes When The Cheers Stop."

Toronto Star; May 16, 2015; Jennifer Morrison," Ex-Leaf Ed Olczyk feels right at home at the racetrack."

Winning the Money Game: Lessons Learned From The Financial Fouls of Pro Athletes; Adonal Foyle. Harper Collins Publishers, 2015

Notes

Notes

Notes